1001 TIPS

for Buying &
Selling a Home

Mark Nash

D1366781

THOMSON
—※—
SOUTH-WESTERN

Australia · Canada · Mexico · Singapore · Spain · United Kingdom · United States

THOMSON
SOUTH-WESTERN

1001 Tips for Buying & Selling a Home

Mark Nash

VP/Editorial Director:
Jack W. Calhoun

VP/Editor-in-Chief:
Dave Shaut

Executive Editor:
Scott Person

Developmental Editor:
Sara Froelicher

Sr. Production Editor:
Elizabeth A. Shipp

Sr. Marketing Manager:
Mark Linton

Manufacturing Coordinators:
Kevin Kluck & Charlene Taylor

Art Director:
Chris Miller

Compositor:
Electro-Publishing

Printer:
RR Donnelley

Table of Contents

Preface

The names change, but the questions stay the same with buyers and sellers of residential real estate. If you have never purchased or sold a home or are ready to move up or scale down, this book is for you. The real estate business has changed considerably since the new millennium, and continues to change daily; the changes make it a more consumer-driven business every day. My clients know that there is no such thing as a dumb question when they work with me. I understand most buyers and sellers lead busy lives during the short or long periods of time between buying and selling their home.

The idea for this book grew out of writing *The Original New Agent's Guide to Starting & Succeeding in Real Estate.* After writing *Starting & Succeeding,* real estate associates and clients suggested I write a book for buyers and sellers, and let them in on the customs, jargon, and shorthand of residential real estate sales. Clients wanted a book written by a full-time real estate agent, because most of them found information by journalists or authors who had not practiced in real estate sales firsthand to be too general.

The purpose of this book is to answer the questions I hear every day from clients concerning the components of their real estate transaction. The components are static, but educating yourself in the personalities and processes will keep you proactive and create a positive real estate experience for you. One reality of real estate that you should keep in mind is that the real estate transaction is the vehicle through which personalities interact. You may think that you have set out to buy or sell your home, but the people who touch the transaction will affect the process for you.

My hope is that the tips that follow will prepare you for the process that lies ahead. These tips and tidbits of advice come out of years of professional experience, learning, and growth. Use these tips to guide you as you proceed with buying and selling real estate.

When you see a symbol, turn to Appendix A for stories of actual circumstances that may help you avoid some pitfalls and make this process rewarding and satisfying.

As smiles appear on my clients' faces, I know we achieved their goal. Purchasing or selling real estate is one of the great investments in life.

1001 Tips for Buying & Selling a Home is my fourth book. These books would never have become reality without the support of the professionals at Thomson Business & Professional Publishing such as Developmental Editor Sara Froelicher, Senior Marketing Manager Mark Linton, and Scott Person, Executive Editor. Special thanks to Doris Barrell, Contributing Editor—she makes writing a pleasure.

This book is dedicated to Linda Brannen and Steve Berg.

About the Author

Mark Nash, real estate author and broker, has published three additional books. *The Original New Agent's Guide to Starting & Succeeding in Real Estate, Fundamentals of Marketing for Real Estate Professionals* and *Reaching Out: The Financial Power of Niche Marketing.* Mark is also a contributing writer for *REALTOR® Magazine Online.* His consumer-centric perspective of residential real estate has been featured on Bloomberg TV.

Mark has been serving real estate consumers for seven years full-time in the Chicago and North Suburban market. He is a broker associate with Coldwell Banker Residential Brokerage in Evanston, Illinois. His sales achievements have included membership in the President's Club and President's Circle. A long-term interest in architecture and real estate inspired him to transition from his career in consumer products marketing and respond to the new expectations of real estate professionals from Internet-based consumers of real estate information.

PART 1
Buying

CHAPTER 1
The Home Purchase Process

1 Take the time to educate yourself about the real estate market in the area where you want to purchase a home.

✔ The purchase of a home is probably the largest purchase you will ever make.

✔ Be sure to include your partner or spouse in the education process.

2 Consider how long it has been since you last purchased a home (if ever).

✔ Most homebuyers don't go through the home purchase process with enough regularity to understand the process until they've closed on their purchase.

✔ If you haven't bought a home in the last five years, you will find that many parts of the home purchase process have changed.

3 Research market conditions in your area.

✔ Real estate market conditions are not static.

✔ Even with interest rates at 30-year lows, in some areas it is still a buyer's market.

✔ Prices in some markets are depreciating.

4 Learn the difference between a buyer's market and a seller's market.

✔ A buyer's market means many properties for sale and few buyers.

✔ A seller's market means many buyers and few properties for sale.

✔ Prices will increase in a seller's market, decrease in a buyer's market.

5 Become familiar with new techniques available today.

✔ You can now apply online for your mortgage.

✔ You can take a virtual tour of a home in which you are interested from the comfort of your home. (At 2 A.M. in the morning in your pajamas!)

✔ You can now retain a "buyer's agent" in most states whose fiduciary responsibility is to you, not the seller. (See Chapter 3, "Working with a Real Estate Agent as a Buyer.")

✔ You can shop for your real estate sales agent online.

✔ You can begin your home search online by visiting consumer multiple listing services.

6 Start your home search by learning about the communities where homes are available for sale.

7 Determine whether the home you are interested in is in a municipality or in an unincorporated area and which county or township it is in.

8 Find out what services, such as fire and police protection, and ambulance service, are provided in the area.

9 Research which school districts serve the new home.

✔ Remember that school districts often change.

✔ Even if you do not have children, schools are an important issue for resale.

10 Check zoning laws for the area.

✔ Will the current zoning laws allow the activities you have planned, such as a home-based business or rental apartment?

✔ What are the plans for nearby open space, such as farm fields or vacant property? Are such areas going to be developed, and if so, how soon and with what type of development?

11 Find out how much the property taxes will be on the home after you pay the purchase price or complete its construction.

12 Expand your real estate vocabulary with the following additional terms:

✔ Real estate: land and its physical improvements.

✔ Real property: ownership rights in land and its improvements.

✔ Contract: a legally enforceable sale agreement to do (or not to do) a particular action.

✔ Notice: a legal announcement.

✔ Insurable title: a clear tile capable of being insured.

✔ Legal description: a description recognized by law that is sufficient to locate and identify property without oral testimony.

✔ Survey: a physical measurement of the area and boundaries of a parcel of land.

✔ Prorations: the division of ongoing expenses and income items, such as property taxes, utility costs, rents, and so on, between the buyer and the seller.

✔ Default: failure to perform a legal duty, such as a failure to carry out the terms of a contract.

✔ Fee simple estate: the largest, most complete bundle of rights one can hold in land ownership.

✔ Warranty: an assurance or guarantee that something is true as stated.

✔ Right of first refusal: the right to match or better an offer before the property is sold to someone else.

✔ Equity: the difference between the current value of a property and the amount still owed on the mortgage.

13 Recognize the various transaction providers involved in the purchase of a home: real estate agent, lender, home inspector, appraiser, insurance agent, title searcher, and settlement attorney. (Each will be described briefly here and in more detail in later chapters.)

14 Learn the role of the real estate agent.

✔ All real estate salespersons must be licensed by the individual state to assist members of the public in the buying, selling, leasing, or managing of real property.

✔ Agents may represent the buyer, the seller, or both in a transaction.

✔ The term *agent* may refer to the salesperson, to a licensed broker, or to the brokerage firm.

✔ A real estate agent with a salesperson's license must practice under the supervision of a real estate broker.

15 Understand the significance of the term REALTOR®.

✔ Members of the National Association of REALTORS®(NAR) are called REALTORS® and are sworn to abide by the REALTOR® Code of Ethics.

✔ A salesperson or broker may be licensed to practice real estate but not be a member of the National Association of Realtors®.

16 Learn the role of the real estate broker.

✔ A real estate broker is licensed by the state with the authority to operate a broker-age firm and is referred to as the principal broker.

✔ Many salespersons also obtain a broker's license, but choose to remain affiliated with another principal broker.

17 Understand the responsibility of a buyer's agent.

✔ A buyer's agent is one who has a signed agreement with a buyer.

✔ A buyer's agent is solely responsible to protect and promote the best interests of the buyer, referred to as the client.

✔ A buyer's agent may be paid directly by the buyer or through the overall transaction.

18 Be aware of the responsibility of a seller's agent.

✔ A seller's agent is also called the listing agent and is someone who has a written agreement with a seller to market property for sale or rent.

✔ A listing agent is solely responsible to protect and promote the best interests of the seller, referred to as the client.

✔ A listing agent can prepare a contract for purchase on behalf of the buyer but has no fiduciary responsibility to the buyer. The buyer is referred to as a customer, not a client.

19 Understand that some states allow dual agency, which requires you to sign a form stating that you have been informed of the dual agent situation and you understand and accept it.

✔ In some states the listing agent can also represent the buyer in what is called dual agency, where the dual agent has equal responsibility to both buyer and seller.

20 Understand the difference between the terms *client* and *customer*.

✔ A client is one, either a buyer or seller, who has a written agreement for agency representation.

✔ All agents have a fiduciary responsibility (a position of trust and confidence) to their clients.

✔ A customer is the other party to a transaction; for example, the seller is the client of the listing agent, the buyer is the customer.

✔ All agents have a duty to be honest in their dealings with customers, but do not have the fiduciary responsibilities due to a client.

21 Inquire about the type of Multiple Listing Service (MLS) provided to real estate agents in your area.

✔ The MLS is either an organization of member brokers agreeing to share listing information and share commissions or an independent company providing information on properties for sale or rent.

✔ Through the MLS system, all agents have access to information about the listings of all brokers participating in the MLS system.

✔ Your agent will be able to show you almost any property for sale in your area.

22 Establish a relationship with a lender early in the home-buying process.

✔ Your offer to purchase will be much stronger if you are already approved for a home mortgage loan.

✔ Mortgage loans may be obtained from commercial banks, savings associations, mortgage brokers, or your credit union.

✔ A home mortgage can also be obtained through an online broker.

23 Shop around for a low interest rate that also has low closing costs.

✔ Comparing the annual percentage rate (APR) is a good way to compare loans offered by different lenders.

✔ The APR discloses the entire cost of the loan, not just the stated interest rate.

24 Be sure to select a company that has a good reputation in the community.

✔ Your real estate agent can provide you with several suggestions.

✔ Friends or family members who have recently obtained a mortgage loan are another good source for a recommended lender.

25 Learn what is meant by being "prequalified."

✔ A loan officer can do a prequalification interview either in person or over the telephone.

✔ A series of questions will be asked about your finances such as employment, income, debt, and funds for down payment and closing.

✔ The answers to these questions enable the loan officer to estimate the amount of a loan that you can afford.

✔ Little of the information, if any at all, is verified.

✔ The advantages of prequalification are that it is quick and involves no cost and little effort.

26 Understand that a prequalification does not offer any commitment by the financial institution to extend credit.

27 Learn what is meant by being *pre-approved*.

✔ For pre-approval, a formal application must be made.

✔ A formal application generally entails meeting with the loan officer in person

✔ A loan application form is completed, a Good Faith Estimate of Closing Costs is reviewed, and numerous disclosures are signed.

✔ Documentation such as paystubs, W-2s, tax returns, and bank statements are submitted.

✔ Information on the application, such as job, income, and money in the bank is verified.

✔ A detailed credit report is prepared.

✔ An underwriter at the financial institution reviews this information and written approval is issued, which is commonly referred to as a Commitment or Approval Letter.

28 Learn how to determine what you can afford to buy.

✔ You will most likely be prequalified by your mortgage broker for more than you are comfortable spending on monthly housing expenses.

✔ See Chapter 4 for more detailed information about mortgages.

29 Decide exactly what your home means to you.

✔ Are you looking for basic housing, the idyllic white picket fence, or your own castle?

✔ Do you see your home mainly as a place to live and enjoy, or as a financial investment?

30 Be realistic about your dreams and goals in buying a home.

✔ We all view our homes from different perspectives, but staying realistic will bring financial rewards and peace of mind after you close.

31 Remember, it may be the first home you buy, but it will probably not be the last.

✔ Your first home gets you started up the ladder of home ownership.

✔ Selling that first home provides funds for a moveup to something larger.

✔ Most people purchase two to three homes in a lifetime.

32 Do not think you must borrow up to absolute maximum when purchasing a home.

✔ Being "house poor" isn't for everyone.

✔ Many people stretch their housing budget to buy the most home they can.

✔ After closing they sit in their dream home and have no extra money in their budget for dinners out, furniture, vacations, college tuitions, or retirement.

33 Learn about the different types of mortgages available.

✔ There are fixed rate, adjustable rate, conventional loans, and government loans.

✔ See Chapter 4 for more detailed information about each type of mortgage.

34 Learn the definition of *mortgage*.

✔ The mortgage is the document that establishes the real property as security (collateral) for the mortgage loan debt.

✔ In the event of default on the mortgage payments, the lender has the right to foreclose on the property, selling it to pay off the mortgage loan debt.

35 Recognize the letters PITI and what they stand for in a mortgage payment.

✔ The P represents the principal, or the amount of the original loan.

✔ The first I represents the interest charged for the use of the principal amount.

✔ The T represents the real property taxes levied by the local jurisdiction.

✔ The second I represents the homeowner's insurance required by the lender, which protects the homeowner from hazard or liability.

36 Read Chapter 4 "Mortgages: What You Need to Know" carefully before making application to a lender.

37 Know what to expect from a home inspector.

✔ A home inspector is a qualified professional who performs an inspection of various home systems and structures.

✔ The home inspector is a generalist, that is, knowledgeable in many areas, but not an expert in all.

38 Locate a qualified home inspector.

✔ Your home inspector should be a member of the American Society of Home Inspectors (ASHI).

✔ Home inspectors must be certified or licensed under trade practice acts in the following states: Alaska, Arizona, Arkansas, California, Connecticut, Georgia, Illinois, Indiana, Louisiana, Maryland, Massachusetts, Mississippi, Montana, and Nevada.

39 Recognize the importance of an inspector being a member of the American Association of Home Inspectors.

✔ ASHI is the oldest and leading nonprofit professional association for independent home inspectors.

✔ Since its formation in 1976, its Standards of Practice have served as the home inspector's performance guideline, universally recognized and accepted by professional and government authorities alike.

✔ ASHI's professional Code of Ethics prohibits members from engaging in conflict-of-interest activities that might compromise their objectivity.

40 Read the following statistics from ASHI and NAR.

NAR & ASHI 2001 Home Inspection Survey Highlights

✔ Of all recent home buyers, 77% obtained a home inspection prior to the purchase of their homes.

✔ A majority of home buyers (57%) personally requested home inspections to be conducted on properties they were in the process of purchasing, while 43% followed their real estate agent's recommendation.

✔ According to REALTORS®, 84% of buyers requested a home inspection as part of the purchase contract.

✔ Nearly all REALTORS® (99%) recommend that the buyer get a home inspection.

✔ Most REALTORS® (84%) have not had any sellers' contracts terminated as a result of an inspection.
Source: American Society of Home Inspectors, "NAR & ASHI 2001 Home Inspection Study," February 2001.

41 Know what to expect from a home inspection.

✔ An examination of the exterior and interior of residential property, including the grounds, the structure, and the mechanical systems, will discover any structural defects; broken or obsolete components; and damage due to water, wear and tear, and other conditions.

✔ The examination should be summarized in a home inspection report.

42 Learn what is contained in a home inspection report.

✔ The report is a written itemization and detailed summation of the findings of the home inspector with regard to the subject property.

✔ The report can be submitted to the seller with requests for repairs or replacements.

43 Anticipate the following typical costs for a home inspection.

✔ Costs may vary for condominiums, single-family homes, and investment properties, such as two and four-unit buildings.

44 Expect to attend the home inspection and to spend several hours with the home inspector.

✔ This inspection is your opportunity to become familiar with all of the technical features of the home.

✔ You will have the opportunity to ask questions of the inspector.

✔ The inspector will be able to point out important features such as water and gas cutoff valves.

45 Do not be surprised if the home inspector asks you to sign a pre-inspection agreement.

✔ The pre-inspection agreement is a contract that protects both the home inspector and the client.

✔ It explains, in general terms, the scope of the inspection (what is included and what is not), the cost, and the procedures to address any dispute that may arise.

46 Understand what is covered in the basic home inspection.

✔ Inspectors look at all structural and mechanical conditions.

✔ Inspection includes but is not limited to foundations, roofs, siding, gutters and downspouts, porches and decks, chimneys, fireplaces, windows, doors, plumbing, electrical, heating, air conditioning, appliances, hot water heaters, pools, interior and exterior walls, and concrete and asphalt surfaces.

47 Learn what is covered in the area of mechanical systems.

✔ Electrical and solar energy

✔ Plumbing

✔ Heating and air-conditioning

48 Be sure that electrical service is adequate to serve your needs.

✔ Most modern homes require amperage of 200 amps.

✔ Your service needs a capacity that will serve all the systems and appliances in your home.

✔ Electric clothes dryers, stoves, baseboard heating, furnaces, air-conditioning, and water heaters all require large amounts of amperage.

49 Learn what is meant by *amperage.*

✔ Amperage is the amount of current or electricity flowing through a wire.

✔ It may be 60, 100, or 200 amps.

50 Determine whether if the main electrical panel contains circuit breakers or fuses.

✔ Updated systems will have circuit breakers.

✔ Fuses are more likely to blow.

✔ Replacing fuses incorrectly can result in a fire.

51 Learn how a circuit breaker works.

✔ The circuit breaker trips and switches off the electrical power for a given circuit if the current increases beyond the capacity of the system.

52 Learn how a fuse works.

✔ A fuse is a device with an internal metal link that melts and opens the circuit, causing electrical power to stop when overheating occurs.

53 Learn how a ground fault circuit interrupter (GFCI) works.

✔ A GFCI is a device that shuts off a circuit immediately if it senses a short circuit, for example, when an electrical appliance is accidentally dropped into water.

✔ Most building codes require GFCIs in all bathrooms.

54 Look to see whether all outlets within 8 feet of sinks or toilets in bathrooms, in the laundry, and on the exterior are ground fault interrupts.

55 Check to be sure all electric outlets have the correct polarity.

56 Discover how electricity is distributed through the home.

✔ Learn whether conduit, romex, aluminum wiring, or knob and tube is used.

57 Learn what is meant by *conduit*.

✔ Conduit is a steel or plastic tube through which electrical wires run.

58 Learn what is meant by *romex.*

✔ Romex is a flexible steel tube through which electrical wires run.

59 Learn what is meant by *aluminum wiring.*

✔ Aluminum wiring is a type of wiring used prior to the 1970s.

✔ It can cause potential fire hazard.

60 Learn what is meant by *knob and tube.*

✔ Knob and tube is an older system of wiring.

61 Understand what is meant by *solar energy.*

✔ Solar energy is radiant energy originating from the sun.

✔ It is popular in climates with a great deal of regular sunshine.

✔ It is often used to heat swimming pools, greenhouses, etc.

62   Observe whether water supply lines are copper, lead, or PVC.

✔ Copper is usually considered to be the best, but it is expensive.

✔ Lead can contribute to lead levels in the water that may be hazardous.

✔ PVC is poly vinyl cloride, which is most often used today due to lower cost and easier handling.

63   Locate a clean out (a pipe fitted with a removable plug to assist in dislodging a pipe obstruction on the main sewer line.

64   Check for good water pressure.

✔ Try running water in a shower and flushing a toilet at the same time.

✔ Turn on outside faucet and kitchen sink at same time.

65   Be sure that the hot water heater is sized properly for number of bathrooms, kitchen, laundry, and special tubs such as a Jacuzzi.

66   Check the age of hot water heater.

67   See that the hot water heater is vented properly to the outside.

68   See whether all water supply lines to fixtures, such as sinks, toilets, and laundry, have shut-off valves.

69   Take notice of whether the home is equipped with a sump pump, and if so, whether it comes with a battery backup system.

70   Check for any smell of sewer gas and be sure that all waste lines are vented properly.

71   If the home you are inspecting is older or has mature trees, consider having a sewer specialist drop a camera into the main waste line that connects to the public sewer in the street.

✔ Over years sewer tiles crack, shift, and can be damaged by tree roots.

✔ Ask the current owner whether they have had the main sewer line rotor-rooted or cleaned out to the street. If they have, ask how often they have had it done.

72 Look for apparent drips, leaks, or water stains in bathroom or kitchen cabinets, basement, ceilings.

73 Learn about different types of heating and air-conditioning systems.

74 Learn how a heat pump works.

✔ A heat pump makes use of a transfer of outside air through a condenser for both heating and air-conditioning.

✔ It is a popular method in new construction.

✔ Works best in more moderate climates.

75 Learn that *radiant heat* refers to heat transferred by radiation, typically found in floors or ceilings.

76 Understand that a boiler system transfers heat from a fuel source to a fluid, such as water, and is constructed from cast iron, steel, or copper.

✔ Known as hot water heat.

✔ Distributed through baseboard or upright radiators.

77 Understand that the word *furnace* refers to any means of heat transfer whether fueled by coal, gas, electricity, or oil.

78 Learn that the term *evaporator* refers to the air-conditioner component that takes heat from the air surrounding it and brings it to the refrigerant.

79 Learn that the *condenser* is an air-conditioner component that liquefies the refrigerant gas by cooling it.

80
Learn that the *compressor* is an air-conditioner component that creates a flow of refrigerant from one part of the system to another.

81
Learn that *refrigerant* is any substance that produces a cooling effect by absorbing heat as it vaporizes (disperses into the air). Freon is a refrigerant.

82
Learn that the British thermal unit (BTU) is a measure of heat energy required to raise the temperature of one pound of water by one degree Fahrenheit.

83
Be able to identify the various structural components of the house (roof, foundation, walls exterior and interior, chimneys and fireplaces, windows and doors.)

84
Find out which type of roofing is on the house: tile, shingle, rolled fiberglass, metal, slate, and wood.

✔ Different types of roofing have different life spans.

✔ Some types of roofing are better suited to a particular environment than others.

85
Learn about the different types of tile used as roofing material.

✔ Clay tile styles, Spanish, French, or flat, are found in a variety of colors and can last in excess of 75 years.

✔ Concrete tile is similar to clay in style; however, concrete tiles weigh less, are less expensive, and can last up to 50 years.

✔ Certain concrete tiles hold up well in cold climates, while others are better suited for areas of the country without the freeze-thaw cycle.

86
Learn about the use of shingles as a roofing material that provides waterproofing integrity for the roof.

✔ Shingles come with various life spans: 20, 25, 30, and 35 years.

✔ The common rule of thumb is that once a roof has three layers of shingles, for the roof to be replaced all three layers must be removed, called a "tear off."

✔ At tear off, roof decking (the wood structure on which shingles are attached) is also checked and replaced as needed, which is an expensive job.

87 **Always look for worn shingles that have curled edges.**

88 **Learn about a fiberglass rolled roof.**

✔ This common material is used on flat roofs.

✔ Roof material is rolled out to cover the roof area, and then seams on adjoining sheets are sealed.

89 **Learn about the use of metal roofs.**

✔ Copper, stainless steel, and tin materials are the most common types of metal roofing.

✔ They provide a long life span, but can be noisy in rain storms.

90 **Understand that even though slate roofs are long-lasting, they are also expensive and difficult to install.**

91 **Recognize that wood/cedar shake roofs are popular and long-lasting, but are also expensive both to install and replace.**

92 **Learn that the roof valley is where two inclined surfaces on a roof intersect.**

93 **Look for examples of various roof styles; gable, hip, reverse gable, shed, and so on.**

94 **Look for roofs that are properly ventilated with ridge and soffit vents.**

95 **Learn that a soffit vent is the perforated area under the roof extension that allows air to flow through the ridge vents to ventilate the attic.**

96 Watch out for roofs that sag in the middle caused by inadequate roof structural support such as rafters, trusses, or ridge beams.

97 Examine skylights (a roof opening that is covered with a watertight transparent cover) carefully for water damage.

98 Learn that *flashing* is a metallic material that is used in certain areas of the roof and walls to prevent water from seeping into the structure

99 Inspect the flashing around skylights for water seepage into the home.

✔ Skylights should not have cloudy glass, a sign that the seal in the window is broken.

✔ In warmer climates the window in a skylight should have a blind to block excessive solar gain.

100 Learn that roof trusses are frames made up of a number of smaller framing members; trusses carry the load-bearing function to the outer walls.

101 Understand the meaning of the term *load-bearing*.

✔ It carries an imposed load.

✔ Exterior and some interior walls of a structure are load-bearing.

✔ Before removing any wall consult with a structural engineer to determine whether a wall is load-bearing.

102 Learn that the rafters are the long wooden framing members that are fastened to the ends of the ceiling joists and form the gables of the roof.

103 Learn that the joists are the wooden framing members used to construct floors and ceilings.

104 Learn that the ridge beam is the highest part of the framing; it forms the apex, or top line, of the roof.

105 Learn that the gable refers to the two ends of the house, or on occasion, to the extension of the attic into projecting window areas.

106 Learn about a slab-on-grade foundation.

✔ The foundation is a concrete slab instead of a foundation wall.

✔ The concrete slab is poured directly on the ground, eliminating the crawl space or basement.

✔ Rooms on slabs can be cold in parts of the country with below-freezing winters.

✔ Slab foundations offer little protection against flooding.

107 Learn what is meant by a *floating slab*.

✔ A type of foundation slab constructed by pouring the footing first, then pouring the slab.

108 Learn that the footing is the concrete base below the frost line that supports the foundation of the structure.

109 Understand what is meant by a full or partial foundation.

✔ Full is one with full adult headroom under the entire footprint of the first floor structure.

✔ Partial has a combination of a full foundation and a crawl space.

110 Learn that the crawlspace is a foundation that does not offer full adult headroom.

111 If the house has a crawl space, make sure a vapor barrier is covered with gravel or poured concrete.

112 Observe whether any moisture or mold is apparent in the crawl space.

113 Learn what a pier is.

✔ This column is designed to support a load.

✔ Some homes on crawlspaces are built on piers.

✔ Beware of wood piers, because the wood could suffer from moisture damage.

114 Understand what is meant by a *walk-out*.

✔ A walk-out provides direct access to the outside of the structure from the foundation level of a home.

✔ A walk-out basement has direct access to the outside.

115 Know what is meant by a *rough-in/stubbed for bathroom*.

✔ When a concrete basement floor is being poured the supply and waste lines for a future bathroom are connected, installed, and capped.

116 Check to be sure that any basement with a poured concrete floor is equipped with floor drains as per building code.

117 Learn the safety requirements for basement windows.

✔ Windows in basements if they are to be used in rooms for living or sleeping must be large enough for an adult to escape in the case of fire.

✔ These windows are called egress (exit) windows.

118 Be aware that low ceiling heights in unfinished full basements can be a negative for some buyers, because they will not be able to build out functional living space.

119 Look for cracks bulges in foundation walls.

120 Look for any phosphorescence (white, shiny fungus-like material) on the foundation or chimney bricks.

121 Learn to identify the various types of exterior walls; siding, brick, concrete, stucco, and wood.

122 Learn about aluminum versus vinyl siding.

✔ Aluminum is more expensive than vinyl, but has a longer life span.

✔ Vinyl siding is prone to fading.

✔ With vinyl siding, dent damage is hard to repair without replacing.

123 Understand that the best benefit of brick walls is durability and longevity.

124 Look for spalling (the crumbling of brick) and the need for tuck pointing (loose or missing mortar between bricks) on older brick walls and chimneys.

125 Watch out for moisture and rotting in masonite or chipboard siding.

126 Be cautious when removing older siding, which may be made of asbestos.

127 Consider the benefits of concrete walls.

✔ Concrete provides a solid hard material produced by combining portland cement, aggregates, sand, and water, and sometimes additives.

✔ All concrete should be sealed against water penetration.

128 Know what is meant by *concrete block*.

✔ This hollow brick of concrete is manufactured to be used in building walls and raised foundations.

✔ All concrete block should be water sealed.

129 Learn the difference between Dri-vit and a stucco wall finish.

✔ Stucco is a Portland cement plaster used as a finish material on building exteriors.

✔ It is preferred over Dri-vit, and is more expensive to install.

✔ Dri-vit is an applied substance, usually over plywood.

130 Examine both pros and cons for wood exterior walls.

✔ Wood is attractive, especially for contemporary architecture or in wooded setting.

✔ It is expensive and difficult to maintain.

✔ It is also prone to rot and fading.

131 Learn about different interior wall materials: drywall, plaster, and paneling.

132 Check the interior walls of the house to see whether they are plaster or drywall.

✔ Older properties are more likely to be plaster.

✔ Most new construction today will be drywall.

133 Learn that drywall is a composite material that is easy to install and looks like plaster when in place.

134 Learn that plaster is a cementitious material, usually a mixture of Portland cement, lime or gypsum, sand, and water, used to finish interior walls and ceilings.

135 Understand that paneling may either be actual wood panels or prefabricated decorative 4' x 8' sheets, installed by attaching it to studs in the wall.

✔ Paneling provides an economical alternative to drywall or plaster.

136 Windows and doors.

✔ Window types: awning, casement (window that opens from the side on hinges), double hung, and slider.

✔ Your home inspector should operate all windows and doors. Windows painted shut pose a fire escape hazard.

✔ Older double hung windows that won't open could have ropes and weights that are broken.

✔ Newer windows that won't open, indicate possible framing or structural problems.

✔ Casement windows crank outward, which is a problem if you want to keep your windows open in the rain.

✔ Insulated or double pane windows help on energy savings.

✔ Fogged windows indicate a leak in the air space between the double panes: the window will have to be replaced.

✔ Make sure you that you can locate all the storm windows and screens at inspection for the home. Replacement cost for storms and screens adds up fast.

✔ All doors to the exterior should have storm and screen doors.

✔ Interior door: hollow and solid core; raised, louvred, and flat panel; Bifold, rolling, and hinged.

✔ Make sure all doors close properly in the jamb which is the vertical member forming the side of a door or window frame.

137 Review the following list of useful life spans (in years) of various home components as provided by the National Association of Home Builders.

Dishwasher	10	Microwave	11	Gas range	19
Electric range	17	Refrigerator	17	Washer	13
Dryer	14	Carpet	11	Cast-iron bathtub	50
Fiberglass bathtub	10–15	Electric water heater	14	Gas water heater	11–13
Ceramic tile countertop	10–15	Laminated countertop	10–15	Exterior door with protected overhang	80–100
Garage door	10	Waterproofing sealer	1–5	Waterproofing silicone	1–5
Waterproofing waxes	1–5	Wall and trim paint	5–10	Exterior paint	7–10
Galvanized ducts	30	Plastic ducts	15	Wood deck	15
Swimming pool	18	Brick wall	100+	Stone wall	100+

138 If the house has automatic garage door openers, be sure that controls are turned over to you at closing.

139 Make sure to locate main shut-offs for natural gas, water, and electrical.

140 Have all circuit breakers or fuses labeled for each area of home served.

141 Find out the location of the hot water thermostat and pilot light on hot water heater.

142 Locate telephone and cable main boxes.

143 Mark the septic clean-out and location of the septic field, if any.

144 Request that sellers leave all appliance, furnace, hot water heater, and other manuals in the house or bring them to closing.

145 Confirm that required smoke and carbon monoxide detectors are installed in your new home and that they operate and are in the right locations for optimal operation.

146 Be sure that you receive a checklist report.

✔ The checklist report itemizes the various components of a property and is organized into sections that allow the inspector to check off inspected property components and comment on any specific problems.

✔ The checklist report may be used to prepare a contingency report requesting certain repairs or replacements from the seller.

✔ The checklist may suggest additional inspections be made to address specific problems.

147 Identify the additional types of inspections that may be suggested.

✔ Chimneys and fireplaces

✔ Swimming pool

✔ Oil and gas tanks

✔ Asbestos

✔ Lead-based paint
✔ Radon
✔ Mold
✔ Septic
✔ Well
✔ Pest/Termite

148 Ask the seller when the last cleaning of all fireplaces and chimneys located in the property was made.

✔ Many people never use a fireplace and it may be full of soot.
✔ The chimney or exhaust pipe for a wood stove should also be cleaned.

149 Observe the condition of the exterior chimney for any loose bricks, apparent leaning, or obstruction at the top.

✔ The brickwork on an old chimney will often need to be recaulked.
✔ Birds often build nests at the top of a chimney stack that is not used frequently.

150 Have an independent chimney inspection done to check the condition of the chimney cap, damper, flue(s), flue collar, and for creosote buildup.

151 Learn that creosote is a black tar-like substance that builds up inside the chimney through normal use and is a common source of chimney fires.

152 Learn that the flue is the enclosed passageway in a chimney or attic through which smoke and other gases move upward.

153 Learn that the flue collar is the opening on the top, rear, or side of a wood burning stove to which the stovepipe is connected.

154 Inquire about any ash pit and how easy is it to clean.

155 Learn that an ash pit is a cavity underneath the firebox that is used as a receptacle for ashes and is accessible through a cleanout door.

156 Learn that the damper is a plate or valve that closes the fireplace flue when the fireplace is not in use, preventing heat loss.

157 Make sure you understand how to use the fireplace damper; which direction is open or closed, or you could have a house full of smoke.

158 Check that a chimney cap covers the top of the chimney to prevent animals from entering the flue.

159 Look through catalogs to decide which type of fireplace appeals most to you: the built-in, freestanding, direct-vent/zero clearance, gas log, gas starter, or wood burning.

✔ Not all homes have the capability to have every type of fireplace.

✔ Many types of gas or electric log fireplaces are available today.

160 Inspect carefully the condition of a swimming pool and surrounding deck.

161 Look for cracks in either the deck or pool.

162 Check for visible staining or algae growth on the interior walls of the pool.

163 Discuss the operation of the pool equipment with the seller.

164 Request copies of all brochures available regarding pool installation and operation.

165 Ask for a record of past maintenance and name of supplier of pool supplies and maintenance.

166 Investigate local ordinances regarding swimming pools: need for fencing, screening, and so on.

167 Make having a certified pool inspection of the pool and equipment a contingency to your contract.

168 Check to see whether the furnace, stove, and other appliances are currently operated by gas, electricity, propane gas, or oil.

169 If either propane gas or oil is used, request an inspection of the storage tank.

170 Inquire as to whether propane gas or oil tanks have ever been on the property.

✔ Many states or local jurisdictions have strict regulations about underground storage tanks.

171 Include the removal of any unused gas or oil storage tanks a part of the contract.

172 Look carefully at exposed pipes in the basement and elsewhere to see whether they appear to be wrapped in asbestos.

✔ Asbestos wrapping was commonly used for insulation in the past.

✔ Asbestos is not a problem if undisturbed.

173 If any asbestos wrapping seems to be peeling or separating, make its removal a contingency to the contract.

174 Look at the tile in basement or other areas to see whether it may be asbestos tile.

175 DO NOT EVER TRY TO REMOVE ASBESTOS YOURSELF!
Disturbed asbestos creates fibers in the air that can damage lungs.

176 Check to see whether the house was built before 1978, in which case lead-based paint is likely to have been used.

177 Be sure that you are given the federally mandated lead-based paint hazard disclosure.

178 Make the removal of peeling paint on properties built before 1978 a contingency to the contract.

✔ Total removal of all lead-based paint may be financially unfeasible but any evidence of peeling should be corrected.

179 DO NOT EVER TRY TO SCRAPE OFF LEAD-BASED PAINT YOURSELF!

✔ The greatest hazard to lead-based paint is when it is disturbed, releasing toxic dust into the air which can damage lungs and neurological systems.

✔ Do not make the mistake of thinking that lead-based paint is only a hazard when ingested; the worst danger is in the air.

180 Include a contingency for a radon test if you have concerns on this issue, especially if you have young children.

✔ Radon is a colorless, odorless, tasteless, radioactive gas present in the environment as a by-product of the natural decay of uranium in the earth.

✔ Much controversy remains about what level of radon is detrimental to health.

✔ Radon levels vary greatly from one locality to another.

181 Do some research on your own about the "hot topic" of the day: mold.

✔ In 2001, the issue of mold and its potential health impact on home purchasers arrived at the forefront of real estate business.

✔ Some lawsuits have been filed over serious cases of mold damage to property and health.

✔ The Consumer Product Safety Commission has issued some guidelines when shopping for a home.

182 Look for rotted building materials that may suggest moisture or water damage.

183 Look for obvious mold growth in attics, basements, crawl spaces, and around the foundation.

184 Make sure downspouts from roof gutters route water away from the building.

185 Look for plants close to the house, particularly if they are damp or rotting. They are a source of biological pollutants.

186 Look for moisture on windows and other flat surfaces.

187 Look for signs of leaks or seepage in the basement.

188 Look for stains on walls, floors, and carpets, including carpet over concrete floors.

189 Check that the kitchen cooktop has a hood vented outside.

190 Check that the clothes dryer is vented outside.

191 Check for exhaust fans in the bathrooms.

192 Make sure all vents lead outdoors and not into attics or crawl spaces.

193 Check that ventless rooms have at least one window that opens to the outside.

194 Hire a professional to check the heating and cooling system, including a humidifier and vents. Have the inspector check duct lining and insulation for mold growth.

195 Look for signs of water seepage behind exterior sheathing. Some homeowners have discovered mold sources behind drywall.

196 Ask whether the house is connected to the public sewer system or is on a septic system.

✔ Some homes outside of urban areas have what is called "private water and sewer" systems.

✔ These systems are located on the property.

197 Ask whether the septic system is conventional, mound, or holding tank system.

198 Learn what is meant by the term *septic system*:

A private household wastewater treatment system consists of a house sewer, septic tank, distribution box, and an absorption field or seepage pit.

199 Learn what is meant by *distribution box*:

Part of a septic system distributes the flow from the septic tank evenly to the absorption field or seepage pits.

200 Learn what is meant by *seepage pit*:

Discharge from the septic tank infiltrates into the surrounding soil through a covered pit.

201 Learn what is meant by *absorption field*:

A system of narrow trenches carries the discharge from a septic tank that infiltrates into the surrounding soil.

202 Learn what is meant by *cesspool*:

Raw sewage collects in a pit (sometimes lined with plastic) composed of stones and gravel. A cesspool is a health and safety hazard and a code violation.

203 Check the local building code that sets minimum construction standards for septic systems in your locality.

204 Ask how old the septic system is. Systems may fail after a period of years.

205 Ask how often the tank is pumped. Yearly is the norm, but frequency may vary according to location.

206 Ask whether the system is sized properly for the home. Septic systems are usually based on number of bedrooms.

207 Take into account the number of occupants in the house.

208 Find out whether the septic system meets the required capacity if additional bedrooms are built.

209 Be aware that owners of private systems are responsible for their maintenance and replacement, if necessary.

210 Keep in mind that unlike public water and sewer, no monthly costs are involved for water and sewer, but costs are high to replace or upgrade systems.

211 Realize that loss of electricity during storms will not allow pumps on wells and some types of septic systems to operate.

212   Recognize that some buyers are reluctant to purchase a home with septic and wells.

213   Ask how deep the well is; this issue can be critical in dry seasons.

214   Ask how many gallons per minute are pumped. This capacity affects water pressure inside the home.

215   Is the well is a drilled? Answer should be yes.

216   Ask what type of pump is used: submersible or other.

217   Ask whether the water in the area is known for high iron or sulfur levels.

218   See whether a water softener system is attached to the well.

219   Ask an inspector whether a water softener system is recommended.

220   See whether the well is used for the total water supply or as a supplement. Sometimes a well is used merely as a backup system or for landscape watering.

221   Have the water tested from a private well for bacteria and all other contaminants as recommended by your county health department.

222   Make both well and septic inspections a contingency to your contract.

223 Learn what is meant by the term *potable water.*

✔ Potable water is safe to drink.

✔ Local jurisdictions have restrictions on bacteria levels in potable water.

224 Learn what a well water storage tank is used for.

✔ A tank prevents the well from pumping every time the household uses water.

✔ Types of well-water storage include pressure tanks, elastic pressure cells, gravity cells, gravity tanks, and reservoirs.

225 Learn what is meant by *pressure tank.*

✔ A well-water storage tank, fills with water and compresses the air inside the tank.

✔ As more water is added, the pressure inside the tank increases because the air takes up more volume. As the water is used, the compressed air pushes the water out of the tank under pressure. As the water level drops in the tank, the volume that the air occupies grows and the pressure exerted decreases.

226 Learn what is meant by *gravity tank.*

✔ A large well-water storage tank is located above the level of the structure.

✔ It differs from other storage tanks because the pressure in the gravity tank is not derived from the amount of water in the tank; rather it is derived from the elevation above the water outlets.

227 If an inspection for termites or other wood-destroying insects is not already required in your standard contract, make your offer contingent on such an inspection by a licensed professional.

228 Request a receipt of the official report on the inspection for wood-destroying insects.

✔ The lender will often require a copy of this report prior to closing.

✔ The inspector should provide at least a one-year warranty.

229 Know what to do if wood-destroying insect damage is found.

✔ In most cases, repairs or replacements required by wood-destroying insect damage must be made by the seller.

✔ In case of controversy, a second inspection may be made.

230 Understand that termites are not the only cause of damage to wood structures.

✔ Other wood-destroying insects are carpenter ants, carpenter bees, and powderpost beetles.

231 For any new contruction or renovation, be sure that a proper building permit has been obtained from the appropriate local government authority.

232 For new construction, do not go to closing until a proper Certificate of Occupancy has been granted by the local government authority.

233 Be able to differentiate between the *appraiser* and the *inspector.*

✔ The appraiser is hired by the lender to determine whether sufficient market value in the property warrants making the requested loan.

✔ The inspector is hired by the purchaser to conduct a general home inspection, or a more specific inspection for environmental issues such as lead-based paint, radon, asbestos, mold, and so on.

234 Understand the role of the appraiser.

✔ The appraiser is licensed or certified by the respective state based on examination, education, and experience requirements to estimate the value of a property.

✔ The appraisal is an estimate of value; the best estimate of the subject property's worth.

✔ The appraiser must be objective, impartial, and unbiased.

235 Recognize the American Institute of Real Estate Appraisers (AIREA).

✔ A professional organization of appraisers.

✔ This professional organization of appraisers unified in 1991 with the Society of Real Estate Appraisers.

✔ Renamed the Appraisal Institute, it is considered to provide the most highly respected designations in the industry.

✔ Designations are the MAI, SRA, and SRPA.

236 Know the value for you to have an appraiser member of the Appraisal Institute.

✔ Members of the Appraisal Institute adhere to a strictly enforced Code of Ethics and Standards of Professional Appraisal Practice.

✔ Members must adhere to canons in their Code of Professional Ethics such as:

✔ Refrain from conduct that is detrimental to their organization, profession and the public.

✔ Develop and report unbiased analyses, opinions, and conclusions.

✔ Must not violate the confidential member-client relationship.

✔ Must not advertise or solicit in a manner that is misleading or contrary to the public interest.

237 Select an appraiser based on the following (In many cases you will not have this option because the appraiser is generally selected by the lender.):

✔ Are they are familiar with the area?

✔ How many appraisals they have done in the area in the last six months?

✔ Are they licensed or certified?

✔ Member of the Appraisal Institute?

✔ How long they have been in business?

✔ Do they work for their own firm or for someone else?

✔ Are they apprenticing?

✔ Are they out of market area or practice somewhere else in the area?

238 Regardless of who selects the appraiser, be sure to ask for a copy of the appraisal letter/report.

✔ The appraisal letter/report is a valuation report in the form of a business letter.

✔ The elements of the appraisal report include:
  • Description of property
  • Location of property
  • Analysis of the highest and best use
  • Analysis of sales of comparable properties
  • Current market activity and market trends

239 Notice the different types of values:

✔ Market value: the cash price that a willing buyer and a willing seller would agree upon, given reasonable exposure of the property to the marketplace, full information as to the potential uses of the property, and no undue compulsion to act.

✔ Insurable value: cost to reproduce or replace the property if destroyed or damaged.

✔ Assessed value: a value placed on a property for the purpose of taxation.

240 Observe how values are determined in three different categories:

✔ Sales comparison: recent sales of comparable properties.

✔ Cost: current cost of reproducing or replacing a building or structure.

✔ Income capitalization: property's net earning power as an investment.

241 Pay the most attention to the sales comparison method of assessing value.

✔ This method is used to compare similar properties, accounting for differences that may affect value.

✔ It is the most common method used to appraise condominiums, townhomes, and single-family homes.

242 See how the cost method is determined.

✔ The land value plus current construction costs minus depreciation determines the value.

✔ Most often used for unique properties such as churches, schools, and so on.

243 Observe how the income capitalization method to value property is based on the monetary returns that a property could be expected to produce.

244
Understand that "highest and best use" means that the use of a parcel of land will produce the greatest current value.

245
If at all possible, request that you have a full-blown appraisal where the appraiser actually enters the property rather than a "drive-by" appraisal.

✔ Some lenders today are satisfied with a drive-by appraisal where the appraiser relies on computerized information.

✔ The drive-by appraisal is most appropriate for refinancing purposes.

246
Recognize that several different types of insurance are involved in a home purchase transaction.

247
Learn what is included in a homeowner's insurance policy.

✔ The lender generally requires that the home be insured against any type of hazard.

✔ The new homeowner should also be insured against any type of liability.

✔ The combined hazard and liability insurance is usually referred to as a homeowner's insurance policy.

✔ The broad form (HO-2) is an insurance policy that covers a large number of named perils.

248
Know what is meant by *mortgage insurance*.

✔ The lender may require a mortgage insurance policy if the down payment is less than a 20 percent of the sales price.

✔ Mortgage insurance protects the lender in case of default on the loan.

✔ Mortgage insurance is paid for by the borrower and usually included as part of the mortgage payment. (PITI plus mortgage insurance.)

249
Understand what occurs in a title search.

✔ An abstractor makes a search of the title history for at least the past 60 years, sometimes longer.

✔ The search is made of all recorded documents pertaining to the property: deeds, liens, wills, and any other legal actions taken on the property.

250 Learn what is covered under the title insurance policy.

✔ The lender will require the new homeowner to purchase lender's title insurance, which protects the property from any future claims up to the amount of the mortgage loan.

✔ The new homeowner should also purchase owner's title insurance to protect the owner against anyone making future claims against the property.

251 Inquire as to how the settlement, or closing, on both the mortgage loan and the conveyance of the property is handled in your area.

✔ In the western states, settlement is handled "in escrow."

✔ In the Midwest and eastern states, settlement is conducted with either a settlement attorney or a title and escrow company agent.

252 Know what to expect at the closing.

✔ Closing "in escrow" occurs when all documents and funds are provided to the escrow agent who then makes the appropriate distributions to all parties involved.

✔ Closing (also called settlement) with a real estate settlement attorney or title and escrow company agent consists of a meeting at which the buyer provides the necessary funds to purchase the property, receives the deed to the property from the seller, and signs all necessary documents required for the mortgage loan. The seller signs the deed over to the new owners and receives payment for the property (usually within 48 hours).

253 Expect to be charged recording fees at closing.

✔ The grantor's or transfer fee is usually paid by the seller.

✔ The buyer will pay for recording of the deed and all mortgage loan liens.

✔ Applicable state, county, and local fees are charged.

254 Take time to make a thorough walk-through prior to closing.

✔ The walk-through is your last chance to check that all systems are in working order and that all requirements for repair/replacement contained in the contract have been satisfied.

✔ Any deficiencies found in the walk-through will be discussed and resolved at closing.

✔ Funds may need to be held in escrow with the settlement attorney to insure that walk-through items are satisfactorily taken care of.

255 Decide whether you would be willing to allow the seller to "rent back" for a period of time.

✔ The seller may feel that some time is needed after closing before leaving the property.

✔ A prorated rent should be charged based on your new mortgage payment.

✔ You should have an additional walk-through at the end of this period.

256 Be able to differentiate between a real estate attorney and an attorney-in-fact.

✔ A real estate attorney is an attorney-at-law that is, a person licensed by the state to practice law who specializes in real estate transactions.

✔ An attorney-in-fact is one who is authorized by another to act in his or her place.

257 Understand the use of a power of attorney.

✔ A power of attorney is a written authorization to another to act on one's behalf.

✔ The power of attorney authorizes one person to sign another person's signature, followed by his (or her) attorney-in-fact.

✔ A power of attorney must be prepared by an attorney.

258 Study carefully each term of the contract, such as purchase price, personal property included in the sale, mortgage contingency clause, inspection clause, prorations, default clause, and warranties.

259 Study the "A" words pertaining to a contract.

✔ Abstract of title: a complete historical summary of all recorded documents affecting the title of a property.

✔ Acceptance: the act of a person to whom something is offered or tendered by another and receives the offering with the intention of retaining it, such intention being evidenced by a sufficient act.

✔ Acknowledgment: a formal declaration before authorized officials (a notary) by a person that he or she, in fact, did sign the document.

✔ Affidavit: a written or printed declaration or statement of facts made voluntarily and confirmed by the oath or affirmation of the party making it taken before an officer having authority to administer such an oath.

260
Take time to make sure that any items of personal property (fireplace screen, riding lawnmower, drapes, microwave, etc.) that you wish to have conveyed with the property are specifically noted and made part of the contract.

261
Never assume that minor repairs or replacements will be made; be sure that everything you wish to have done is included as a condition of the contract.

262
Review all terms of the contract to be sure that the contract does not favor the other side.

263
Make sure that all required disclosure forms are attached to the contract.

✔ Most states require a disclosure of agency or brokerage relationships.

✔ Many states require a property disclosure listing any known defects.

✔ All states require a lead-based paint disclosure for properties built before 1978.

✔ Some jurisdictions have special disclosure requirements regarding soil conditions, energy costs, flood liability, and many other issues.

264
Ensure that any inspection and attorney review periods are for a typically short period of time after acceptance, and once the period expires, that no additional changes can be made.

265
Be prepared to receive a counteroffer to your original offer to purchase.

✔ The seller has the option to accept your offer to purchase as stated in the contract, or to reject it totally.

✔ The seller can also make a counteroffer, which in effect cancels your original offer and is now an offer to sell that is extended to you.

266
Plan ahead for how you will respond to a counteroffer.

✔ You, the buyer, now have the option to accept, reject, or counter the counteroffer.

267 Have a real estate attorney review your real estate purchase contract before you sign.

✔ This review is a good idea even if you are in an area where it is not common to have attorneys involved in the home purchase/sale transaction.

268 Study carefully the following list of issues that your real estate attorney can assist you with throughout the transaction from contract acceptance to closing.

✔ Check for errors in figures.

✔ Look for any errors in documents.

✔ See that mortgage contingency terms are met according to contract; deliver notice if contingency cannot be met under contract terms.

✔ Negotiate any final walk-through issues.

✔ Review of title search and can request something to be struck or insured.

✔ Ensure that the buyer is purchasing the correct property through legal description.

✔ See that the title is clear, and taxes and liens are paid.

✔ Review the property survey.

✔ Review the mortgage and note, as well as all mortgage lender documents.

✔ Protect the buyer's rights with regard to the lender.

269 Take into consideration these important reasons for having an attorney involved in your home purchase.

✔ Despite what you may think, real estate agents and mortgage lenders do not look out for your legal interests.

✔ Your real estate broker and lender are not typically compensated if the transaction does not close.

✔ It is unlikely real estate agents or mortgage lenders will call attention to potential problems that could jeopardize their commissions.

✔ Unless you hire an attorney, your legal rights in a property purchase or sale could be diminished.

✔ Non-attorneys are not trained or experienced in legal issues surrounding the conveyance of real property.

270 Learn what to expect from your real estate attorney.

✔ The duties of a real estate attorney for buyer and seller include reviewing and discussing contract with client, making recommendations based on a client's objectives, conveying changes or suggestions in writing to other attorneys, reviewing and discussing inspection items with client, communicating with other attorneys in writing, and attending closing.

✔ Duties for just the buyer include following progress of mortgage; requesting additional time, if necessary, for unconditional commitment; and explaining lender documents and seller documents at closing.

✔ Duties for just the seller include ordering title search, survey, and, if property is a condo, certain condominium papers, as well as payoff letter, and preparing all documents to transfer title.

✔ The attorney should communicate with the client regularly regarding all steps in the procedure.

271 Look for an attorney who specializes in real estate law.

272 Find an attorney who is familiar with the contract and required disclosures in the area where you will be buying or selling.

273 Find an attorney who understands condominium and cooperative declarations, bylaws, right of first refusal, and rules and regulations if you are planning to purchase or sell a condominium.

274 Do not be afraid to "shop around" for an attorney.

✔ Base your choice of attorney on references and other research, not solely on charge per hour.

✔ Unless you anticipate severe problems, you may not need the most highly paid attorney in town.

275 Be aware of possible problems if an attorney does not review your contract before it is signed.

✔ A modification letter from your attorney after signatures could create a counter-offer.

✔ A counteroffer can cancel your original real estate contract.

✔ You may end up with no contract to buy or sell.

276 Listen to your transaction service providers.

✔ They are the experts.

✔ If you disagree with their advice or lose confidence in their actions, find new ones.

277 Take your time. Do not let anyone rush you.

✔ You have the right to ask all the questions that you wish.

✔ You should read carefully every document that you are asked to sign.

278 Be sure you feel comfortable and confident with your decisions.

✔ Home ownership is not for everyone.

✔ Consider both short-term and long-term goals.

✔ Never feel that this something that you *must* do at the present time.

279 Do not wait too long to purchase a home.

✔ The longer you rent, the longer you will have no control over your housing expenses.

✔ If you receive a fixed-rate mortgage for your home purchase, inflation will only impact your property taxes and homeowners insurance, not the principal and interest portion of the payment.

280 Observe the following apples-to-apples housing comparison:

✔ You pay $800 per month in rent for a two-bedroom house, which does not include heat or electricity.

✔ You purchase a home for $90,000 putting 10% as your down payment and borrowing $81,000.

✔ $81,000 at 7% interest equals a P and I payment of approximately $538.90.

✔ Property taxes are approximately 1.5% of purchase price ($90,000) which equals $1,350 ($112.50/month) plus $250 ($20.83/month) for homeowner's insurance.

✔ $538.90 + $112.50 + $20.83 = $672.23.

✔ In this scenario, the mortgage payment is actually less than the rent.

281 Keep the right priority in mind; first things first.

✔ Find a mortgage.

✔ Find a real estate agent.

✔ Find a real estate attorney.

✔ Find a home inspector.

282   Drive through a community at different times of the day to get a feeling for the overall ambiance of the community.

✔ In the morning when residents are going to school or work.

✔ During the day to see whether properties are maintained, including alleys.

✔ At night to check on traffic noise, parking availability, and lighting.

283   Walk or bicycle through areas to get a slow look, include schools, playgrounds, and parks.

284   Talk to local store and shop owners.

285   Find out whether stores and restaurants are open late at night if you need to run out for milk or a prescription.

286   See whether you can easily group errands for efficiency or services are spread out.

287   Attend school and village board meetings to understand what local issues are.

288   Visit the library to see whether their collection is thorough enough for you and your children, read some issues of the local newspaper.

289   Surf the Internet for community-related Web sites.

290   Visit the police station and inquire about crime statistics and neighborhood watch groups.

✔ In some states, you may also search online to learn whether a sex offender lives in the neighborhood.

291 Consider the following locations carefully both for yourself and for eventual resale.

✔ Resale potential of home on a busy street, next to railroad or mass transit tracks, or commercial buildings may be lower.

✔ In some instances, homes across from schools, swimming pools, and large playgrounds take more time to sell.

292 Learn what is meant by the term *condominium*.

✔ Condominium is a form of ownership, not a physical description of property.

✔ A condominium is most often seen as an apartment-like building, but can also be townhouses, or even single-family detached houses.

✔ A Declarations/Master Deed establishes a parcel of land as a condominium subdivision.

✔ The bylaws are the rules that govern how an owners' property association will be run.

293 Learn what is obtained when purchasing a condominium unit.

✔ A condominium is individual ownership of a single unit in a multiple-unit structures (or structures) with common elements.

✔ Ownership in a condominium unit consists of a fee simple interest in a specific unit with an undivided interest in all common elements.

294 Understand the role of the condominium Homeowners Association (HOA).

✔ The HOA provides a legal framework so that condominium unit owners can govern themselves: to control, regulate, and maintain the common elements for the overall welfare and benefit of its members.

✔ The HOA is a mini-government by and for condominium owners, which can be organized as a trust or unincorporated association; most often it will be organized as a corporation in order to provide the legal protections normally afforded by a corporation to its owners.

✔ The HOA will be organized as a not-for-profit so as to avoid income taxes on money collected from members.

✔ A unit purchaser is automatically a member.

✔ The HOA levies monthly, quarterly, or annual assessments for the upkeep of all common elements.

✔ Nonpayment of condominium assessments will result in a lien on the property.

295 Learn what is meant by the term *cooperative.*

✔ A cooperative is a building owned or leased by a corporation, which in turn leases space to its shareholders through a proprietary lease.

✔ Ownership of shares in a cooperative venture entitles the owner to use, rent, or sell a specific unit.

✔ Most cooperative boards require a personal financial statement at application.

✔ Buyer interviews by the association board are typically required.

✔ Property taxes are included in monthly or quarterly assessments.

✔ Ownership of a cooperative is different from owning a condominium, because it is not a fee simple interest in a specific unit.

✔ Financing for a cooperative is often more difficult to obtain than that for a condominium unit.

296 Learn what is meant by the term *townhouse.*

✔ A townhouse is usually a dwelling unit of two or three floors and shared walls; most often found in a planned unit development (PUD).

✔ A townhouse is attached to several other homes, usually in a section of 7–10 properties.

✔ Attached homes were historically referred to as row houses.

297 Understand what is meant by the term *planned unit development (PUD).*

✔ A PUD consists of individually owned lots and houses with community ownership of common areas.

✔ A monthly or quarterly assessment is made to cover maintenance of common areas.

298 Understand the difference between a *duplex* and *semi-detached* home.

✔ A duplex is one building with two separate living units. (Triplex is three.)

✔ Semi-detached means two separate units attached with a common wall.

299 Learn what is meant by the term *manufactured home.*

✔ A manufactured home may be anything from a double-wide trailer to a two-story Colonial home.

✔ A prefabricated manufactured home is when the sections of the house are prepared in an off-site factory location and then assembled on site.

✔ Manufactured housing is defined by the U.S. Department of Housing and Urban Development as a dwelling that contains at least 320 square feet with a permanent chassis to assure the initial and continued transport of the home.

✔ Many manufactured homes are placed on foundations and not mobile at all.

✔ The Manufactured Housing Institute states on their Web site that federal standards and written warranties protect buyers of manufactured homes.

✔ Manufactured homes are inspected during construction in order to meet home construction and safety standards.

300 As you would any other home purchase, have your manufactured home inspected by a qualified home inspector.

301 Be aware that you can buy a home without the services of a real estate agent.

✔ If you are undecided about purchasing a home and want to take your time, look at many homes, and not have an agent driving your home search, you might prefer to work on your own.

✔ Dealing directly with listing agents and for-sale-by-owners can give you a first hand learning experience.

✔ You need to understand that you cannot purchase a home listed in the local Multiple Listing Service (MLS) without the assistance of a broker member of the MLS.

✔ If you do buy without an agent, you might consider hiring a good attorney to write and review the contracts.

302 Be prepared to answer the following questions the first time you meet with a real estate agent.

✔ What kind of home are you looking for? Desired features such as age, eat-in kitchen, family room, fenced-in yard, fireplace, garage/parking, location, neighborhood, number of bedrooms, bathrooms, price range, size/square, footage, style, updated.

✔ What is your time frame to purchase?

✔ When are you free to look at potential properties?

✔ Are you renting or do you need to sell before you buy?

✔ Do you work at home or are you otherwise self-employed?

✔ Have you talked with a lender?

303   Tell your agent if you are a first-time buyer.

✔ It will help them understand that you will need education and at times some hand holding; all homeowners have been there!

✔ Remember though to have reasonable expectations, understand current market conditions, and listen to the counseling your agent gives you.

304   Take into consideration the pluses for renting versus owning:

✔ *Monthly costs*: Renting can be more cost-efficient than owning if utilities are included. The monthly cost of owning is usually more than renting after you total the cost of mortgage, maintenance, taxes, and utilities.

✔ *Features*: Some rental apartments offer amenities that are not found in smaller condo/co-op buildings or single-family houses such as 24-hour door attendant, dry cleaners, or a grocery store. Unless you purchase in a full-amenity building you will most likely have to go off-site for some services you are accustomed to having only an elevator ride away.

✔ *Maintenance and repairs*: Renting allows you the luxury of repairing or maintaining nothing; if the air-conditioner breaks you call the manager. With owning you have to either repair the air-conditioner yourself or locate, meet, and pay a repairperson.

✔ *Mobility*: Renting offers you the convenience of leaving your home when your lease expires. When owning you are tied to other persons' timeline of moving when a buyer or a tenant agrees to a date, which might not fit your timeline.

305   Take into consideration the pluses for owning versus renting:

✔ *Equity*: Renting has no equity benefits. Owning provides a forced savings because part of each monthly payment is principal, which builds your equity. Potential property appreciation can also increase your equity. *Note*: If property values decrease in your market you could owe money when you sell.

✔ *Control over your environment*: A lease may not allow you to have pets, paint your walls red, or have a roommate. With owning you can choose a building or home that allows you to have pets, decorate to your taste, have roommates, or add a washer and dryer.

✔ *Stability*: Your landlord can increase your rent, sell the property, or convert your rental to condos and force you to move on short notice. With a fixed-rate mortgage, you can control your monthly housing expense and peace of mind that you can stay as long as you want.

✔ *Tax benefits*: Renting offers none. Owning allows you to deduct mortgage interest and home equity interest from your taxable income. Consult a tax professional for more information.

306 Recognize that renting might be a better option for you in the following situations:

✔ If you are in a life transition, such as recently widowed or divorced, it will offer you flexibility.

✔ You do not wish to have repairs or maintenance responsibility.

✔ You have alternative investments for your down payment funds.

✔ If you frequently travel for business or pleasure, renting gives you the freedom to lock up and go away, worry and responsibility free.

✔ Your company is considering relocating you in the next 20 months.

✔ Your company is considering downsizing its employees, merging with another company, or selling to new ownership.

✔ The real estate market you want to buy in is a seller's market, major employers are leaving town, or uncertainty about proposed development could affect housing prices in a negative way.

307 Look for the following when at home showings.

✔ Does the home draw you in, or push you away?

✔ Do you like the room flow and sizes?

✔ How about the decorating? Wallpaper can mask wall issues. Fresh paint on basement walls and floors might be covering water stains.

✔ Is the home in good condition?

✔ Does the home smell of pets, tobacco, or dampness?

✔ Are the rooms filled with natural light? Many people today want high levels of natural light in all rooms. View homes during daylight hours.

✔ Are the hardwood floors in good condition? Any signs of water leaks or stains? Does the house have "good bones," quality workmanship and materials?

✔ Can you visualize yourself living there? Can you put your furniture in the space?

✔ Lift area rugs to inspect floors underneath.

✔ Large artwork or mirrors, bookcases, and other large furniture can cover wall problems. Is the house evenly heated or cooled?

✔ Does the basement or crawl space smell musty or have water stains or evidence of water seepage?

✔ Homes speak to us, so take a good listen.

308 Take the following items with you on home showings.

✔ Listing sheet

✔ Camera, always ask if you can take pictures of a home you're viewing

✔ Note-taking materials

✔ Tape measure

✔ Flashlight

309 Pay attention to the following considerations to ensure good resale value.

✔ The more bedrooms, the greater number of buyers your home will appeal to at resale.

✔ Two or more bathrooms appeal to most homebuyers.

✔ Upgraded kitchen and baths are of primary interest.

310 Observe whether the kitchen has a place for eating.

✔ Most buyers minimally want a breakfast bar in the kitchen to eat a meal on the run or have a cup of coffee.

✔ Although dining rooms are popular, most families never eat in them!

311 Look for walk-in closets and adequate overall storage space, especially if the house has no basement.

312 Check for available storage space: basement, attic, outside shed, extra closets.

313 Walk through the home observing the following for room flow:

✔ Are rooms arranged off central hallways?

✔ Do you have to walk through rooms to get to other rooms?

✔ Are the bedrooms away from living spaces for noise considerations?

✔ Can you get to bathrooms from bedrooms without going through living spaces?

✔ Is there a master bath?

✔ Is the garage attached or detached? (Many buyers like the convenience of going directly from the garage into their home.)

✔ Have additions disrupted room flow?

✔ Are bathrooms located on each level in a multilevel home?

✔ Will you be constantly on the stairs in a more vertical home?

314 Make a list of attractive home amenities.

✔ Laundry: Is it near bedrooms?

✔ If condo or co-op, is there an in-unit laundry?

✔ Fireplace(s): Wood burning or gas logs?

✔ Garage: Large enough for your vehicles and storage?

✔ If no garage, is off street parking available?

✔ Fenced yard: For keeping pets and young children out of harm's way?

✔ Central heat and air-conditioning? A must-have for most home buyers today.

✔ Hardwood floors? Growing in popularity with buyers.

✔ High-speed Internet and cable?

✔ Phone jacks spread throughout house?

✔ Deck, patio, or balcony?

315 Recognize the impact of a swimming pool on resale value.

✔ In warmer clients, buyers appreciate this feature.

✔ In colder clients, a pool is an expensive buyer issue to remove.

316 Determine which of the following describes the house location.

✔ Corner lot (faces two streets)

✔ Interior building (in row of houses)

✔ End unit (end of townhouse row)

✔ Cul-de-sac (street closed at one end with circular turnaround)

317 Recognize the difference in waterfront and water view descriptions.

✔ Waterfront means the property is adjacent to a large body of water.

✔ Water view means a property that has views of water but is not adjacent to water.

✔ A water view is subject to change with the season.

✔ Some properties that have water views have water rights.

318   Learn the difference between riparian rights and water rights.

✔ Riparian rights are the right of a landowner whose land borders a river, stream, or lake to use and enjoy that water.

✔ Water rights are the right to use water on, below, or bordering a parcel of land.

319   Keep in mind the importance of property location for resale value.

✔ The ability to walk to schools, shopping, and public transportation all rank high on buyers' wish lists regarding location.

✔ Most buyers would prefer a quiet cul-de-sac over a busy street.

320   Consider asking the sellers to provide you with a home warranty.

✔ This feature acts basically as an insurance policy that provides you with repair or replacement service on appliances and in some cases, on heating and cooling equipment and the roof.

✔ The policy ranges from $350 to $500 in most areas and includes a deductible amount.

321   Take into consideration how you wish the property title to be held: joint tenancy, tenancy-in-common, or tenants by the entirety.

✔ With joint tenancy, title passes to the survivor when one owner dies.

✔ In tenancy-in-common, the deceased party's interest passes on to heir.

✔ Tenants by the entirety is reserved for married couples and is not available in all states.

✔ Severalty is the name for property held in one person's name solely.

Chapter 2
Your Search for a New Home

322 Establish your parameters for your new home.
✔ Lifestyle
✔ Schools
✔ Investment
✔ Resale
✔ Shelter
✔ Proximity to work
✔ New(er) with no major remodeling or updating required
✔ Dated, tired, or needs tender loving care (TLC)

323 Determine whether lifestyle is your motivation to purchase a home.
✔ Do you define who you are by where you live?
✔ Do you spend the majority of your free time at home?
✔ Do the style and features of a home need to complement your personality?
✔ Do your home and community need to make a statement about you to your friends, family, or business associates?

324 Recognize that the quality and location of your children's schools could drive your home selection.
✔ Do you prefer certain school districts?
✔ Do your children need extracurricular programs?
✔ Do you want a strong college preparatory curriculum?
✔ Do you have a special needs child?
✔ Are your school needs more important than home parameters?

325 Remember to factor your pet's needs in your home selection.

✔ If you are buying a condo, verify that the building allows pets and which types, the maximum number of pets allowed, and if any weight limits for pets exist.

✔ Do your pets need a fenced backyard or dog run?

326 If you are buying in a rural area that is becoming suburban, verify that you can have horses or other animals that might not be allowed in the near future if development increases.

327 Find out if you will be buying in a home market that experiences consistent recent appreciation of home values.

328 Recognize that you can also be looking for your housing to be an investment.

✔ What is the annual rate of appreciation? For how many years in a row?

✔ Should you consider two- or four-unit apartment buildings where tenants help fund your mortgage payments?

✔ Is there strong demand at resale for your investment property?

329 Anticipate the probability of good resale characteristics of any home you are considering to purchase.

✔ Does your new home fit typical style and size requirements of most buyers in your market?

✔ Are potential homes under consideration the same age and condition as the norm for the community?

✔ Does your new home's location have a typical location away from busy streets, fire stations, hospitals, and other noise and site-related issues?

✔ Will buyers of your home at resale be attracted to and motivated to make it their home?

330 Realize that your first home might provide shelter, appreciation, monthly housing cost consistency, but might not be your dream home.

✔ Will your first home provide a platform to move up in the housing market?

✔ Will deferring a home purchase in your market possibly price you out of the market in the future?

✔ Are you looking for a starter home to build equity?

✔ First-time home-buyers stay in their home an average of 5.9 years according to the National Association of REALTORS® 2002 Profile of Home Buyers and Sellers.

331 Research the viability of purchasing a foreclosed or repossessed property if you are on a tight budget.

✔ Typically, foreclosed and repossessed properties are in distressed condition.

✔ Some auctions featuring foreclosed or repossessed properties require that you purchase the property with no inspections.

332 Ask real estate agents who is the contact person for foreclosed properties.

333 Review real estate advertising to find out the location of foreclosed properties.

334 Decide if your home needs to be convenient to work, schools, and services.

✔ Will long and difficult commutes to work, schools, or services diminish your enjoyment of your new home?

✔ Do you want to be near public transportation?

✔ Do you want to walk to work, parks, shopping, or services?

335 Check out crime statistics for your new neighborhood.

✔ Ask the local police department what the statistics were in the previous five years.

✔ Are crime rates headed up or down?

336 Consider purchasing a home warranty for your new home if you are concerned about unexpected repairs to systems or appliances.

✔ Covered items in standard home warranty policies: heating system, heat pump, air-conditioner, ductwork, plumbing system, sump pump, whirlpool tub, water heater, electrical system, exhaust fan, dishwasher, garbage disposal, built-in microwave oven, range/oven/cook top, trash compactor, garage door opener, and ceiling fan.

✔ Optional additional coverage for these items: washer/dryer, refrigerator, well pump, swimming pool, or spa equipment.

✔ The standard policies are $400—$500 for one year.

✔ Copayment of $60 per service call or repair.

✔ Home warranties can be utilized when property inspections discover that some appliances or systems are near the end of their useful life.

337 **Ask your real estate agent to provide you with several home warranty programs that are popular in your area and the cost for each program.**

338 **Decide how much work you are willing to do on a home you purchase.**

✔ Do you have the time, financial resources, and skills to remodel kitchen and bathrooms?

✔ Do want a home that is updated and requires little of your time and money?

✔ Do you want a new house, where you can select finishes throughout?

✔ Do you have the time for minor projects such as painting and hardwood floor refinishing?

339 **If you are considering a single-family home, determine whether you have the time for exterior routine maintenance such as lawn moving, landscaping, snow shoveling, painting, and window cleaning. If you travel out of town frequently, who will perform these functions?**

340 **Educate yourself about new home construction.**

341 **Research developers at your local library before you purchase.**

342 **Check complaints with the local Better Business Bureau about a developer you are considering.**

343 **Ask friends and relatives if they know anyone who has purchased directly from the builder.**

344 **Have an attorney review any developer contracts before you sign.**

345 **Learn that a developer is a company, group, or individual who adds to the value of land by installing improvements on it.**

346 **Remember to ask your builder to provide you with a Certificate of Occupancy (CO) at closing or escrow for your new home.**

✔ The CO is a document issued by local government that indicates a structure meets all local zoning and building codes and is ready for habitation.

347 **Bring the real estate agent you are working with the first time you visit models at a new construction development or rehab.**

✔ Typically agents must register you on your first visit or they loose the opportunity to be paid a commission by the builder for representing you.

✔ If you have a signed buyer agent agreement, and purchase a new home without using the services of the buyer agent, you may still be liable for a commission.

348 **Familiarize yourself with the different types of housing.**

✔ Single-family home
✔ Condominium
✔ Cooperative apartment
✔ Townhouse, Row house
✔ Duplex
✔ Manufactured home

349 **Learn that the definition of a single-family home is a dwelling with no common walls with another dwelling unit.**

350 **Become familiar with the various styles of single-family homes.**

✔ One-level home style terms: cottage, ranch, rambler, and bungalow.

✔ Two-story home style terms: A-frame, Georgian, Cape Cod, Colonial, contemporary, English Tudor, French provincial, Mediterranean, Queen Anne, Victorian, and farmhouse.

✔ Multilevel homestyle terms: bilevel, split level, trilevel, and raised ranch.

✔ Manufactured home.

351 Know the definition of a Homeowners Association (HOA)

✔ A legal framework created by by-laws and declarations to govern, control, regulate and maintain the common elements for the benefits of its members.

352 Be aware that Homeowners Associations charge assessments to cover the costs of administration of and maintaining the association.

353 Recognize how an assessment is a fee charged to the member homeowner in exchange for services provided to the homeowner by the association.

354 Understand that homeowner association or condominium assessments are not tax deductible.

355 Understand what is included in your condominium assessment.

✔ Heat

✔ Air conditioning

✔ Water

✔ Electric

✔ Gas

✔ Parking

✔ Common insurance

✔ Security

✔ Security system

✔ Door attendant

✔ TV/Cable

✔ Club house

✔ Exercise facilities

✔ Pool

✔ Exterior maintenance

✔ Lawn care

✔ Scavenger (trash pick-up)

✔ Snow removal

✔ Management fees

356 Realize that property taxes are included in cooperative assessments.

357 Find out when your assessment is due and how it is paid.

✔ Monthly

✔ Quarterly

✔ Annually

358 Determine whether any special assessments are due or proposed for the condominium you are considering purchasing.

✔ Capital improvements: New parking lots or exercise rooms.

✔ Renovation: New hallway and lobby décor.

✔ Replacement/repairs: New windows, roofs, or balconies.

359 Ask for copies of the condominium declarations, bylaws, two-years' budgets, and association meeting minutes from the preceding six months immediately after you have an accepted contract to purchase a condominium unit.

360 Find out from the association's budget how much is in its reserve fund.

361 Be aware of the meaning of a reserve fund.

✔ Monies set aside from assessments each year to replace systems or fixtures that are part of the common elements.

✔ Limited reserves could result in additional assessments.

362 Learn what the common elements of your condominium or townhouse in an homeowners association are.

✔ Roof

✔ Windows

✔ Siding

✔ Balconies/patios

✔ Walkways and porches

363 Study the different terms related to condominiums.

✔ Common area/grounds: The elements of building and grounds that all unit owners own jointly.

✔ Condominium: A dwelling of two or more property units where the owner owns the interior space and, in common with other owners, owns a square foot ratio of the common areas, such as the grounds, hallways, stairways, lobby, mechanical systems of common areas, and parking and recreational areas.

✔ Cooperative (co-op): A corporation in which the tenants purchase shares that give them the right to occupy a unit in the building.

✔ Courtyard: An outdoors space faced by a building.

✔ Duplex: Two properties joined by one common wall.

✔ Elevator building: One that has one or more elevators to reach the units.

✔ Flat: Another name for an apartment.

✔ Full-amenity building: One that offers a variety of services to occupants: door attendant, delivery/shipping room, dry cleaner, pool, tennis court, store, exercise facilities, and so on.

✔ Garden apartment: A dwelling unit partially below grade.

✔ High-rise: A multiple-floor building of 10 or more floors.

✔ Management company: A professional real estate management company that manages the physical operation of a building.

✔ On-site management: The building management personnel who work from an office within the building.

✔ Parking:

Deeded: A parking space owned as a piece of real estate

Leased: A parking space leased by the building occupant

Underground: A parking space located beneath grade of the building

Assigned: A parking space appointed by the association or management company

Valet: Service in which a parking attendant parks the vehicle for the occupant of the space.

✔ Self-managed: Buildings and dwelling units overseen by unit owners or unit shareholders.

✔ Site engineer: The mechanical or operations professional for a building who is onsite at his or her place of employment. Some engineers live on the premises and are referred to as the super, short for superintendent.

✔ Walk-up: A building with no elevator.

364 Be aware of other property terms that you might hear during your home search.

✔ Income/investment property: Property that provides compensation or tax advantages to the owner.

✔ 2–4 units: A multiple-dwelling building of two to four units.

✔ 2/3 flat: A multiple-dwelling building that has two or three units stacked on top of each other.

✔ Lakefront: A dwelling unit that has front footage on a lake.

✔ Lake view: A dwelling unit that has visual exposure to a lake.

✔ Manufactured home: All or part of a dwelling unit that is constructed in one location and placed in another location.

✔ Midrise: A multiple-floor building that has three to nine floors.

✔ Mobile home: A dwelling unit that is constructed with attached wheels and can be moved from one location to another.

✔ Model home/condo: A dwelling unit that the builder/developer finishes as a sales sample for the public to view.

✔ Penthouse: A dwelling unit of the highest occupied floor of a building.

✔ Percent owner-occupied: The number of units in a condo or co-op that are owner–occupied.

✔ Rental: Property for which the occupant/tenant pays the landlord/owner a fixed periodical sum of money.

✔ Riparian: Property rights relating to land bordering flowing water.

✔ Row houses: Attached homes with a common side wall(s).

✔ Quadrominium: Four attached condominiums.

✔ Spec home: A home built on speculation by a builder/developer.

✔ Studio: A one-room dwelling unit.

✔ Townhouse: A series of attached dwelling units with common wall(s).

✔ Vacation or resort or second home: A residence owned as a nonprimary residence.

✔ Water rights: Rights by a property owner to use a body of water.

365 Study new construction terms you might hear in a new development.

✔ Allowance

✔ Option

✔ Package

✔ Proposed

✔ Standard

✔ Stubbed bath
✔ Upgrade

366 Understand air-conditioning terms.

✔ Central air
✔ Space Pac
✔ Evaporator
✔ Window/wall
✔ Zoned

367 Become familiar with basement and foundation terms.

✔ Block: Concrete
✔ Brick
✔ Cellar: A room for storing garden products (i.e., bulbs, canned goods, and so on)
✔ Concrete
✔ Crawl space: A shallow space beneath the first floor
✔ English: One that is partially above grade
✔ Exterior access: One that has a door to the outside
✔ Finished: One that has drywalled or paneled rooms
✔ Full: One that is the same size as the first floor, excluding the garage
✔ Partial: One that does not cover the same area as the first floor
✔ Partially finished: One that has drywalled or paneled walls
✔ Piers/pillars: Supports under a dwelling unit
✔ Slab: A concrete slab foundation
✔ Stone: Stone as side walls of foundation
✔ Unfinished: One that has no finished space
✔ Walk-out: One that has a door to the outside
✔ Wood: One that has side walls or the floor constructed from wood

368 Recognize bathroom terms you will hear during home showings.

✔ Master
✔ Full
✔ Powder
✔ Jack and Jill

✔ En suite

✔ Shared bath

369 Examine different fireplace options you could have in your home.

✔ Decorative

✔ Electric

✔ Gas logs

✔ Gas starter

✔ Heatilator

✔ Wood-burning

370 Have all fireplaces and wood-burning stoves inspected by a chimney specialist and cleaned annually.

✔ Look for signs of creosote buildup in the flue.

✔ Creosote: A black tar like substance that is a residue from burning wood and can cause chimney fires.

✔ Flue: An enclosed passageway in a chimney through which smoke and gases pass upward.

371 Research which heating fuel type is best for your home.

✔ Baseboard

✔ Electric

✔ Gas

✔ Gravity air

✔ Forced air

✔ Heat pump

✔ Hot water/steam

✔ Oil

✔ Propane

✔ Radiant

✔ Radiators

✔ Solar

372 Become familiar with the term British thermal unit (BTU) in heating systems.

✔ A unit of measurement of heat energy required to raise the temperature of one pound of water by one degree Fahrenheit.

373 Understand the meaning of r-value when applied to insulating materials found in homes.

✔ The degree of resistance to heat transfer through walls. The larger the resistance, the greater is the R-value.

374 Research different types of roofing materials.

✔ Asphalt rolled
✔ Asphalt shingles
✔ Copper
✔ Fiberglass rolled
✔ Fiberglass shingles
✔ Metal
✔ Rubber
✔ Slate
✔ Tar and gravel
✔ Tile
✔ Tin
✔ Wood shakes/shingles

375 Decide which additional rooms you would like in your home.

✔ Artist's studio
✔ Craft or hobby room
✔ Darkroom
✔ Den/office/study
✔ Exercise room
✔ Foyer
✔ Gallery
✔ Great room
✔ Greenhouse

✔ In-law arrangement
✔ Lanai
✔ Library
✔ Loft
✔ Maid's room or nanny's quarters
✔ Porch, enclosed
✔ Porch, screened
✔ Recreation room
✔ Sitting room
✔ Workshop

376 Review the list of additional rooms you would like to have in your new home and see if there are ways to make double use of the same space (i.e., exercise room and recreation room; craft or hobby room and artist's studio; den/office and library; etc.)

Chapter 3

Working with a Real Estate Agent as a Buyer

377 **Decide what you want most from your real estate professional based on the following suggestions:**

✔ Help in finding the right house to purchase

✔ Help with price negotiations

✔ Help with paperwork

✔ Information on what comparable homes are selling for

✔ Information on how much you can afford

✔ Help in finding and arranging financing

378 **Compare your choices with this national survey:**

What Buyers Want Most from Real Estate Professionals

✔ Help you find the right house to purchase 57%

✔ Help with price negotiations 11%

✔ Help with paperwork 11%

✔ Tell you what comparable homes are selling for 10%

✔ Tell you how much buyer could afford 7%

✔ Help find and arrange financing 4%
Source: 2003 National Association of REALTORS® Profile of Homebuyers and Sellers.

379 **Ask your employer whether your company has a relationship with a relocation company.**

✔ If so, they should be able to provide you with real estate agent referrals.

380 **Check with your friends and family to see if they can recommend an agent.**

381 Do some research on the Internet:

✔ Check out http://www.realtor.com.

✔ Visit brokerage and agent Web sites.

382 Contact your last agent for a referral if you are moving to an area that company does not service.

✔ Click on the Web site for the city to which you are moving to see whether REALTORS® are listed.

✔ Call three real estate firms and ask the managing broker for agent referrals.

✔ Visit public open houses and get to know agents in the market you will be purchasing in.

383 Pick which resources you think will be most helpful for you from the following list:

Real estate agent *86%*
Yard sign 69%
Internet 65%
Newspaper 49%
Home book/magazine *35%*
Open house *48 %*
Builders *37%*
Television *22%*
Relocation company *14%*

Source: 2003 National Association of REALTORS® Profile of Homebuyers and Sellers.

384 Read the following home buyer statistics from the *2003 National Association of REALTORS® Profile of Homebuyers and Sellers* to see how the Internet may be helpful for you.

✔ Nearly three out of four home buyers now use the Internet as a tool when searching for a home.

✔ Those who use the Internet are more likely to use real estate professionals: 90% of Internet searchers used a real estate professional, compared to 79% of nonInternet users.

✔ 41% of buyers learned about their home from a real estate agent, 16% first learned about their home from yard signs, and 7% learned about their home from the following: newspapers, builders, or friend, family, or neighbors.

✔ 63% of home buyers said the Internet shortened the search time for their new home.

385   Compare yourself with the typical Internet-user home buyer today.

✔ A typical Internet home buyer is a married 38-year-old, with household income of $70,700.

✔ A typical non-Internet user homebuyer is a married 47-year-old, with a household income of $56,300.

Source: 2003 National Association of REALTORS® Profile of Homebuyers and Sellers.

386   See if you fit the "typical repeat buyer" statistics.

✔ The typical repeat buyer is a married 46-year-old, with a household income of $74,600, and puts down 23% on a home of $189,000.

Source: 2003 National Association of REALTORS® Profile of Homebuyers and Sellers.

387   Do not feel obligated to work with an agent who you worked with on a previous real estate transaction unless you are comfortable with the following:

Mark's Stories

✔ Does the agent communicate and listen to you well?

✔ Do you have compatible personalities?

✔ You will spend a minimum of three to six months working with this person.

✔ Your expectation should be to have a reasonably pleasant experience purchasing a home.

388   Do not work with an agent new to the real estate business.

✔ Would you trust your largest consumer purchase to a rookie?

✔ New agents are great for showing properties, but lack the seasoned negotiation skills to get you the best terms for your new home.

389   Do not work with a part-time agent.

✔ Finding your home and going to a successful closing takes a full-time effort from your real estate agent.

✔ You need schedule flexibility from your agent, hearing that they can't show you a home because they have "to work" indicates your home purchase is not a top priority for them.

390 Insist on working with the real estate agent, not their assistant.

✔ Your agent needs to be with you through the entire process as the buyer processes evolve. If they're not around they can miss important turning points in your home search.

✔ An assistant is fine for administrative work, but you need a seasoned agent for 90% of your home purchase transaction.

391 Do not necessarily choose to work with a top producer.

✔ Top producers usually don't have enough time for all their clients because they are so busy producing, that the majority of their work goes to their assistant.

392 Look for a consistent midlevel producer who has the time to work for you and is usually service and detail oriented.

393 Do not feel obligated to work with a family member or friend who is a real estate sales agent.

✔ You will most likely be either selling or purchasing your largest asset, your home.

✔ It is not a time to feel indebted to working with anyone you do not feel comfortable with.

✔ If your brother's girlfriend or your uncle Bert approaches you to help with your real estate needs, interview them like you would any other real estate professional.

✔ It might help if you don't want to use family or friends to say, "We decided not to use family/friends in our real estate search, so we don't alienate those we don't use."

394 Work with one agent at a time in your home search.

✔ If you are working with an agent, tell the agents that you meet that you have an agent.

✔ License laws in some states prohibit agents from soliciting potential clients that already have an agent.

✔ One excellent agent is better than three who know that you are loyal to none.

✔ Real estate agent communities are small and well connected; word spreads fast when buyers have multiple agents.

✔ Working with one agent minimizes procuring cause issues.

395 Learn the meaning of *procuring cause.*

✔ This claim is made by a buyer's real estate agent that the foundation for negotiation and the consummation of the sale would not have taken place without his or her efforts.

✔ It becomes important when two agents are in dispute over who actually sold you the property.

✔ To avoid getting caught up in this type of dispute, work with only one agent.

396 Insist that your agent show you all available properties for sale, not just the properties listed with their company.

✔ You want to see all available property no matter who is representing it.

✔ Some companies give incentives to agents for the sale of a listing when agents represent both the seller and the buyer from the same company.

397 Remember, the choice of an agent is yours, even if they are part of a team.

✔ If you are not comfortable with other members of your agent's team, you do not have to work with them.

✔ Discuss with your agent that you would like to work exclusively with them as part of your buyer's representation agreement.

398 Feel free to discuss your concerns when your agent and the agent representing the seller are from the same office or company.

✔ Discuss your concerns with your agent if you feel a conflict of interest exists in this in-house sale.

✔ Contact the managing broker and discuss your concerns with them.

✔ This situation is not considered a dual agency, because the sellers have a listing agreement with their agent and you have a buyer's representation agreement with your agent. The listing agent has a loyalty to his or her principal, the seller, just as your buyer agent has to you.

399 Recognize the term *in-house* sale.

✔ In-house sale is when a sale is made by an agent from the same real estate office that acquired the listing of the sold property.

400 Understand your role as the principal.

✔ A person who authorizes another to act for him.

401 Demand your right as a principal to the transaction to have loyalty from your agent.

✔ Agency law and the Code of Ethics require that an agent place a principal's interest above his or her own.

402 Be willing to meet your agent at the office before being shown property for the first time.

✔ Agent's concerns about safety with meeting clients they don't know at properties, have prompted brokerages to encourage having clients come to their office for the first meeting with an agent.

✔ Agents have been attacked and murdered while showing vacant properties to clients they haven't met.

403 Be prepared to have photo identification available to your new agent.

✔ Do not be offended when asked. It is a safety precaution.

404 Take the time to meet the managing broker while you're in the office.

✔ It is a good opportunity to meet the manger. If you have problems later, you will have a face to go with the name.

405 Go to your first meeting with the agent prepared with financing information.

✔ If you have not been prequalified by a lender before meeting with the agent, be prepared to go through this procedure.

✔ Prequalifying will help determine an appropriate price range home to look at.

406 Learn why you need to be a qualified buyer.

✔ A buyer who has gone through the process of being qualified for a loan is in a much stronger bargaining position with a seller.

✔ In a case of multiple offers on the same property, the candidate with the strongest financial position has the greatest advantage.

407 Be honest with your agent about how much you are willing to spend on a property.

✔ When you start your home search tell your agent what you are *comfortable* spending on a home. You might be approved for more, but disclose that you are not comfortable spending that amount.

✔ Contrary to public perception, most professional agents want you to be confident and comfortable with all your home-buying decisions, so you should not experience pressure to move beyond your comfort price level.

✔ The difference in commission for the extra $5,000 in sale price is negligible. Depending on their commission split with the broker, on a 5% commission an agent will receive between $62.50and $93.75 on the $5,000 in additional sales price.

408 Recognize the term *commission split*.

Mark's Stories

✔ The percentage split of commission compensation between the real estate sales brokerage and their real estate sales agent are individual and vary according to an agent's agreement with the company.

✔ People often think that the agent receives the entire commission shown on a closing statement; on the contrary, it is almost always split with the company.

✔ In the case of "100 percent" companies, such as REMax, the agent does receive the entire commission but must pay rent and other costs to the broker.

409 Ask for clarification if your agent uses real estate jargon that you don't understand to describe home purchase transaction terms.

✔ Knowing some basic real estate terms could make your communication more efficient with your agent.

✔ Every business has its own "lingo"—do not be ashamed to ask what something means.

410 If your agent will not show you homes in a neighborhood that you have an interest in, find a new agent and familiarize yourself with Fair Housing Law.

✔ License law commits agents to show you any neighborhoods or communities you request to see. If your agent refuses to show you available homes in communities or neighborhoods, that could be construed as steering, which is against the Fair Housing Law.

✔ The illegal practice of steering means directing home seekers to, or away from, particular neighborhoods based on race, color, religion, sex, national origin, handicapped, or familial status (adults-only).

411 Do not be angry or distressed if occasionally your agent is not able to accompany you to a public open house.

✔ Agents sometimes have to sit their own listings for public open house.

✔ Take advantage of the flexibility you'll have without an agent.

✔ Visiting solo should only happen occasionally, not as a regular practice.

412 Take the following actions when you visit an open house on your own.

✔ When you sign in, tell the agent hosting the open house that you are working with an agent.

✔ Resist any pressure from the listing agent to have you sign a contract.

413 Be aware that not all agents hosting public open houses are the listing agent for the property.

✔ New agents often host public open houses for experienced agents.

✔ Experienced agents use public open houses to prospect for new clients.

✔ If the agent doesn't seem to know basic property details, they most likely are not the listing agent.

414 If you have interest or questions about the property, ask your agent to contact the listing agent.

✔ Too much discussion with the listing agent could lead to an eventual question of procuring cause if the listing agent felt that he or she was the one who actually sold you the house.

415 When your market is a strong sellers' market, ask your agent if you can go with them on broker's tour.

✔ Most Boards of REALTORS® have a designated day each week when new or existing listings are open for brokers to preview for clients.

✔ The broker's tour is a good way to see properties before they have wide exposure to other buyers.

✔ Usually your agent must accompany you on a brokers' tour .

✔ Some agents enforce "brokers only," and will not allow clients.

416 Learn the difference between a sellers' market and a buyers' market.

✔ You will hear or read about these terms as both a reason and an excuse for current market conditions.

✔ In a sellers' market, few properties are for sale, with many buyers. This situation obviously affects price and the sellers' willingness to provide any concessions.

✔ A buyers' market, means many properties are listed for sale, but few buyers are looking to purchase. Buyers are in a good position to negotiate lower prices and ask for concessions from the seller.

417 Stop wondering what your buyer agent is doing when not showing you property. An agent's daily activities include much more than showing houses.

✔ Agents spend time and marketing expense to receive buyers' calls and/or e-mail.

✔ Some agents take regular floor duty time answering incoming calls to the office.

✔ Agents attend office sales meetings on a weekly or monthly basis.

✔ Agents attend company sales/award meetings.

✔ Continuing education and professional development courses are a must for agents.

✔ Agents take time to prepare buyers' packets for meeting to show property.

✔ Actual time is spent meeting with first-time prospective buyers.

✔ More time is spent meeting with prospective buyers along with mortgage lenders.

✔ Appointments must be made to preview properties.

✔ Actually previewing potential properties for buyers.

✔ Attending brokers open houses to view new inventories of homes for sale.

✔ Making appointments to view potential properties with buyers.

✔ Accompanying buyers looking at potential properties.

✔ Writing contracts, preparing disclosure forms, and so on for buyer's prospective property to purchase.

✔ Delivering and presenting contracts to sellers' agent and sellers.

✔ Negotiating terms of contract until agreement is reached.

✔ Counseling buyers through negotiation.

✔ Courier contract to buyers for sign off on changes as agreed upon in negotiation.

✔ If the property is a condo or part of a property owners' association, agent must procure and deliver condo declarations, bylaws, rules, and application.

✔ Preparing brokerage worksheet for transaction.

✔ Contacting and forwarding contract to attorneys, escrow agent, and mortgage lender.

✔ Attending property inspections.

✔ Negotiating property inspection issues.

✔ Communicating contract status to buyers, attorneys, and escrow agents.

✔ Accompanying buyers on property showings to measure, meet contractors, or show property to friends and family after the contract is ratified.

✔ Making ongoing assorted phone calls and sending e-mails to participants in the transaction.

✔ Preparing required brokerage documents for closing.

✔ Setting up and attending final walk-through before closing.

✔ Attending closing.

✔ Purchasing and delivering client thank-you gift.

✔ Assisting buyers with movers, repairs, and other related details.

✔ Posting closing follow-up with buyers.

418 **Appreciate that your agent spends time previewing property.**

✔ Previewing takes place when a buyer's agent views a property without the clients to see whether it meets his or her buyer's needs.

✔ This service can save you a great deal of time and energy, because the agent can eliminate those properties that are not what you are looking for.

419 **Know that the time your agent spends on the office tour/caravan is important to you.**

✔ The caravan is a walking or driving tour by a real estate sales office of listings represented by agents in the office. It is usually held on a set day and time, typically after the weekly sales meeting.

✔ Your agent may see a property on this tour that meets your needs before it actually appears on the general market.

420 **Learn the meaning of the following terms relative to condominiums.**

✔ The condominium bylaws: rules passed by the condominium association that are used in the administration of the condominium property.

✔ Condominium declarations: a document that legally establishes a condominium.

✔ Condominium rules and regulation: rules of a condominium association by which owners agree to abide.

421 Be aware of the importance of timeliness in purchasing a condominium.

✔ In most states, a set period of time allows you to review all of the condominium documents.

✔ If you are not satisfied with the documents, you are allowed a set number of days in which you can void the contract.

✔ Failing to act in a timely manner could force you to purchase a unit in a project that you are not satisfied with.

422 Be sympathetic to tenants' right when you are being shown the property in which they presently live.

✔ Some states may have actual law; in all cases, it is courtesy to give 24 to 48 hours' notice before showing the property.

✔ Realize that the tenants may be unhappy with having to move and not inclined to be cooperative.

423 Take advantage of your right to have a final walk-through of the property.

✔ The walk-through is a final inspection of the property just prior to settlement.

✔ The property should be in substantially the same condition as on the day that you signed a contract to purchase.

424 Take the following actions on your walk-through:

✔ See that any repairs, removals, or other stipulations that were agreed upon in the contract have been successfully completed.

✔ Turn on all appliances and check to see that they are in working order.

✔ Check HVAC (heat and air-conditioning) systems.

✔ Flush toilets and check for leaks in the sinks.

✔ Run the garbage disposal (if any).

✔ Run the washer and dryer through one cycle.

✔ Check electrical outlets.

✔ Verify that all of the seller's property has been removed.

425 Ask your agent to show you how the lockbox (or key box) works. Use of a lockbox is limited to members of a REALTOR® association. Different types of lockboxes include:

✔ Supra-electronic lockbox that requires keypad to gain access to keys

✔ NAR's new lockbox

✔ Push button lockboxes

✔ Combination lockboxes (The combination lockbox is sometimes used for entry by workers, inspectors, and others who do not have REALTOR® access.

426 Become familiar with market customs regarding showing of property in your particular market area.

✔ In some areas, all showings must be scheduled with and accompanied by the listing agent.

✔ In other areas, any member of the REALTOR® association with a lockbox key can gain access to the property. A courtesy call should be made to the seller in advance of the showing.

427 Remember that your agent knows your home needs from previous showing experiences better than the listing agent.

✔ If the listing agent is not allowing you to see the property at your order, pace, or

discretion, ask your agent to inform the listing agent that you would like some time to take in the property uninterrupted.

428 Limit the listing agent's input to information that is not readily obvious during the showing.

✔ Some properties have special features that might not be visible to the buyer, let the listing agent explain these, thank them, and continue on at your pace.

✔ Long-winded listing agents should not be a barrier to your quick exit from a property that doesn't work or a tight home tour schedule.

429 Don't allow listing agents to follow you around saying "This is the kitchen," "This is the dining room," and so on.

✔ Listing agents either need to add value or remain quiet and in the background.

✔ You may be able to circumvent these obvious comments by asking specific questions about the property or the neighborhood.

430 Take time to check out the location of the house and the neighborhood, perhaps driving around several blocks before viewing the house.

✔ Remember that you will live in the whole neighborhood, not just inside your house.

✔ A smaller house in a neighborhood of larger homes is usually a good investment.

✔ Having the biggest and best house on the block is not generally a good idea.

431 Check with the local police department if you want crime statistics.

✔ Real estate agents are restricted by Fair Housing laws in the type of information they can give to a prospective purchaser to avoid any incidence of "steering" someone to, or away from, a specific property.

✔ Each state has specific requirements for the dissemination of information regarding released sex offenders who live in a neighborhood (Megan's Law).

432 Locate the nearest shopping center, schools, church, recreation facilities, and any other sites that are important to your family's life style.

✔ The number of miles is not as important as the ability to get to the desired location easily and safely.

✔ Times open and any admission costs should be verified.

433 Spend some time at the property in order to observe the amount of vehicular traffic and any presence of railroad or airplane noise.

✔ Too many people have been unpleasantly surprised after moving in by the roar of a passing train or airplane taking off or landing.

✔ The listing agent's standard answer will be "Oh, you get used to it!" Maybe so, but do you want the house badly enough to put up with the nuisance?

434 Observe whether bus or subway service is located nearby.

✔ Even if you do not need such service yourself, it will have an impact on the traffic near your home.

✔ Proximity to transportation can also be an important consideration at whatever time you wish to sell the property.

435 Be sure to observe what is across the street from the house.

✔ You will spend more time looking out of your front windows than you will spend standing outside looking in.

✔ If the view presently includes a lovely lake or wooded area, be sure to inquire what any future plans are for that property.

436 Watch for signs of young children in the neighborhood such as ride-on toys parked in the driveway, swing set in the backyard, or playhouse in a tree.

✔ This feature may be important to you if you either want, or do not want, a neighborhood with many children.

✔ If you want a neighborhood with young children, the proximity of schools will also be important.

437 Do not hesitate to ask the neighbors about the local schools.

✔ Individual parents will be able to tell you more about the schools than your real estate agent who is restricted by Fair Housing laws.

438 If your children are very young, do not be overly concerned about the quality of the local high school.

✔ The school districts may be changed by the time your children are that age.

✔ Different schools have different areas of expertise. At this point in time, you do not know whether you will be looking for a high school that has a great sports program or one that specializes in fine arts or advanced placement courses.

✔ The odds are good that you will have moved again before your children are ready to enter high school.

439 Walk through both the front and back yards checking to see whether the lawn, shrubs and other plantings look well cared for.

✔ The condition of the outside is often an indicator of the amount of care taken inside.

✔ Soggy or marshy areas may indicate a drainage problem.

✔ Shrubs or woodpiles located near the house may present a termite problem.

440 Ask yourself honestly whether it is a yard that you will happy to maintain.

✔ That beautiful flower garden will not tend itself.

✔ A full acre of lawn will require lots of mowing.

✔ Those lovely trees have leaves that will require raking come fall.

✔ That gorgeous circular driveway will need plowing in winter.

441   Decide what you want most in your yard.

✔ Are you looking for space for a garden?

✔ Do you need a fenced area for a dog?

✔ Do you prefer a yard mostly open to the sunshine or one that will provide shade?

✔ Is there room for a swimming pool if you want one?

442   Pretend you are someone coming to visit your new home.

✔ What will be their first impression of the house?

✔ Were you proud or apologetic about the place?

443   Take a few minutes before actually entering the home to look at the condition of the front door, adjacent windowsills, the soffit (the underside of a roof overhang), and porch rails.

✔ Peeling paint may be evidence of a moisture problem

✔ Mold can also indicate a moisture problem.

444   Close your eyes for a moment then open them as you step into the house.

✔ What is the first thing that catches your attention?

✔ Does it feel crowded or cramped?

✔ Does it feel inviting?

445   As you move through the rooms of the house, pay attention to the amount of natural light.

✔ More buyers' today demand homes filled with natural light.

✔ Large windows will provide the light but will also require window treatments, which can be expensive.

446   Observe the flow pattern from one room to another.

✔ Are the rooms arranged in an order that will work for your family?

✔ If you interested in the Asian concept of *feng shui* the flow of energy (*chi*) throughout the house will be important.

447 Take careful note of the overall floor plan.

✔ Buyers are sometimes overwhelmed with the beautiful living room and forget to make sure some other place such as a family room is available for the kids to hang out.

448 Be realistic about the number of bedrooms you need.

✔ If the rest of the house were perfect, would two children be willing to share a room?

✔ If the fourth bedroom is to be used for a computer room, could that be done in the basement, making the three-bedroom house acceptable?

✔ Could the den or family room double up as an occasional guest room?

✔ Although three bedrooms are fine for now, are more children anticipated, or parents who will need to move in the near future? Better to plan ahead.

449 Be willing to overlook deficiencies that are only cosmetic.

✔ A stiff scrub brush and a coat of paint will do wonders.

✔ The house merely needing TLC may be a bargain as long as it has no structural or irreparable defects.

450 Look for telephone and cable jacks throughout the house.

✔ Are the antenna or cable hookups in the room where you want the TV?

✔ Is the house ready for DSL (high-speed Internet)?

✔ Are telephone jacks located in the bedrooms, kitchen, or other places you will need phones?

✔ Of course these hookups can be added after move-in, but it is a plus to have them already in place.

451 Stand in the kitchen and pretend you are preparing a meal.

✔ Is there an easy flow between the sink, stove, and refrigerator?

✔ Is there adequate cabinet space for your dishes and pots and pans?

✔ Is there enough open counterspace to place small appliances plus leave working room?

✔ Will the appliances need updating? If so, how soon?

✔ Is there eating space in the kitchen or will it always be necessary to use the dining room?

452 Measure the dining room carefully.

✔ Grandmother's antique china cabinet may not fit in this space.

✔ Does the room permit extending the table for special occasions?

✔ Does it allow enough room for your oriental rug?

453 Pay special attention to the bathrooms.

✔ Older homes generally have fewer, and smaller, bathrooms.

✔ Is there room to enlarge a bathroom to fit the Jacuzzi you want?

✔ Could a powder room be added on the main level?

✔ Are the fixtures outdated and in need of replacing?

✔ It is not easy, and usually expensive, to add bathrooms.

454 If your dream home is a lovely old Victorian, be prepared to compromise.

✔ Are you willing to trade off modern bathrooms for large rooms with high ceilings?

✔ Can you make up for limited closet space by turning a small room into a walk-in closet?

✔ Will you be satisfied to use an armoire in lieu of a closet in the master bedroom?

455 If you want hardwood floors and the house is fully carpeted, check bedroom closets.

✔ Most people do not carpet the floor of a closet.

✔ Sometimes you can slightly pull up an edge of the carpet to see the condition of the floor underneath.

✔ If hardwood floors are especially important to you, make your contract contingent on a full inspection of the floors. (Carpet hides many mishaps.)

456 Ask the sellers if they have, or have had, pets in the house.

✔ Pet "accidents" may have left damaged spots in the carpet or floor.

✔ Pet odors often linger after the pet has moved out.

✔ Make your contract contingent on having the house treated for fleas and ticks.

457 If you or someone in the family suffers from allergies you will want to have a thorough home inspection.

Mark's Stories

✔ Will you have to replace all the wall-to-wall carpet because of an allergy to cat dander?

✔ Evidence of mold can be a severe problem, especially for a child with asthma.

✔ Do trees in the yard present a pollen problem?

✔ If the sellers are smokers, extra cleaning and/or painting may be necessary.

458 Take the following items along with you when you preview a home.

✔ Note-taking materials

✔ Camera

✔ Tape measure

✔ Flashlight

✔ Your agent should provide you with the Multiple Listing sheet.

459 Inform your agent if you are allergic to pet dander and hair at the beginning of your home search. Tell your agent that you cannot view homes with cats or dogs because of allergic reactions.

460 Allow yourself plenty of time for your home search.

✔ Statistics show that the median amount of time for a home search is eight weeks.

✔ In a "hot" market with few listings and multiple offers, you may have to make offers on several properties before one will be accepted.

✔ In a "slow" market with many homes of sale, you will have the luxury of taking longer to make a decision.

461 Plan to look at enough houses that you will satisfied with the one you choose, but do not expect to see everything that is for sale in a given market (unless only two or three homes are available.)

✔ The average number of homes seen is 10.

✔ Your real estate agent will help you pick out the available properties that best match your wish list.

462 Select a well-qualified buyer's agent to assist you in the home search.

✔ You can buy directly from a home builder, but you will not have the benefit of a buyer's agent who will be protecting your best interests.

✔ The buyer agent is paid through the transaction, not directly by you.

✔ Every agent has access to all of the homes listed in the local Multiple Listing Service.

✔ 75% of home sales are made through an agent, 14% from the builder, and 9% direct from the previous owner.

✔ 74% of buyers said they would use the same agent again.

Source: 2003 National Association of REALTORS® Profile of Homebuyers and Sellers.

463 Try doing your own research at http://www.realtor.com or other home search Web sites.

✔ It's fun to do and will give you an overall picture of the market.

✔ You can contact an agent right from the Web site or take your selections with you to the agent you have chosen to work with.

✔ 72% of buyers visited a home that they had viewed online.

✔ 18% found their agent through the Internet.

Source: *2003 National Association of REALTORS® Profile of Homebuyers and Sellers.*

464 Unless you are in a "hot" market area, do not feel pressured to write a purchase agreement after a showing.

✔ If you need some time, use the old "I'd like to sleep on it."

✔ You will feel more confident in the purchase agreement when you have not been hurried into it.

✔ It is usually a good idea to revisit the property prior to making an offer.

465 Take as much time as you need: overnight, a couple of days, or a week.

✔ Not writing a purchase agreement *immediately* after a showing may provide you with more negotiating power. (You do not appear overanxious.)

✔ Do understand that you run the risk of the property being sold to someone else while you are making up your mind.

466 Ask your agent to explain the process of making an offer to purchase in your area.

✔ A purchase agreement is not the same as a real estate contract in some localities.

✔ In New York and a few other areas, the agent prepares a letter of intent, or a binder. An attorney must draw up the contract.

✔ In most areas, the real estate agent fills in the blanks in a offer to purchase form usually provided by the local association of REALTORS®.

467 Understand the importance of signing a contract.

✔ A contract is a legally enforceable agreement to do (or not to do) a particular thing.

✔ Once you have signed a purchase contract and it has been accepted by the seller you are legally obligated to fulfill the terms of the contract.

✔ Any effort to bow out of the agreement will be considered a breach of contract, which is punishable by law.

468 Learn how to protect yourself by using contingencies.

✔ A contingency is added to a contract and states that some action must either be taken, or not taken, or the contract will become void with no penalty.

✔ A typical contingency is on the purchaser being able to obtain financing at the terms described in the contract.

✔ Contingencies may also be for a variety of home inspections, sale of another property, removal or inclusion of items on the property, or anything else that is important to you.

✔ The seller does not have to accept your proposed contingency and may reject the contract but at no penalty for you.

469 Be prepared to write a check for an earnest money deposit to accompany your offer.

✔ Depending on local custom, earnest money checks are made out to either the listing or the selling broker's firm.

✔ If the listing broker is a one-person office or has not been in business long, have your own agent's firm hold the earnest money.

✔ If you are purchasing a home from an unrepresented seller, have your agent's firm or the attorney representing the sellers hold the earnest money.

470 Do not try to get by with a small earnest money deposit.

✔ The money that accompanies an offer to purchase is given as evidence of good faith to carry out the terms of the contract.

✔ When a seller has multiple offers on a property, the one with the largest earnest money deposit will often win out.

✔ The earnest money deposit is not an extra charge; it will credit to the purchase price at settlement.

471 Take extra care if you are attempting to purchase a property from an unrepresented seller.

✔ An unrepresented seller is one who does not have a signed listing agreement with a licensed broker.

✔ The unrepresented seller is familiarly known as a for-sale-by-owner (FSBO).

✔ You will need a real estate attorney to assist you when purchasing from a FSBO.

472 Do not allow your agent to arbitrarily waive any contingencies you have included in your purchase contract.

✔ In a hot market, it will be tempting to waive contingencies for financing or appraisal in order to make your offer more attractive.

✔ If you waive the contingency for either obtaining financing or having an appraisal and are not able to go through with the transaction, you will be subject to lawsuit.

473 Always make your offer contingent of having a home inspection.

✔ If your market is so hot that this contingency will kill any chance of having your offer accepted, you might need to reconsider.

✔ In normal circumstances, having the home inspection is very important.

474 Learn what to expect from a home inspection.

✔ A home inspection is an examination of the exterior and interior of residential property including the grounds, the structure, and the mechanical systems to determine structural defects; broken or obsolete components; and damage due to water, wear and tear, and other conditions.

✔ The purchaser pays for the home inspection at the time of the inspection.

✔ Rates vary throughout the country but generally range between $250 and $500.

475 Do not expect the home inspector to be an expert in all fields.

✔ The home inspector is considered to be a generalist; in other words, the inspector knows a lot about many aspects of the home but is not an expert in all areas.

✔ If the home inspector spots a potentially serious problem, a further inspection by an expert will be recommended.

476 Understand what happens as a result of the home inspection.

✔ As a condition for removal of the home inspection contingency, you will request the seller to make certain repairs, replacements, or other action.

✔ The seller has the option to agree to take care of all of the listed items, agree to do some part of the list, or refuse to do anything.

✔ You will have the option to accept the seller's choices or declare the contract void.

✔ Prior to settlement you have the right to make an inspection to see that the agreed-upon items have been taken care of.

477 Learn the difference between home inspection items and those found at the final walk-through.

✔ Home inspection items are basically a request for action, which the seller can either accept or refuse.

✔ You are entitled to a final walk-through of the property just prior to settlement.

✔ The property is to be in substantially the same condition as when you made the offer to purchase.

✔ Most contracts include a paragraph that states that all appliances and systems must be in working order.

478 On the final walk-through, make sure that all storm doors, windows, and screens that were present at the time of contract are still there and unbroken.

✔ Open and shut all doors and windows.

479 Turn on all appliances and run through one cycle.

480 Check all electrical and phone outlets.

481 Turn on heating and cooling systems if possible.

✔ Depending on the season, it may not be possible to check one or the other.

482 Ensure that any specific items you included as part of the contract have been accomplished.

483 Know what to do if problems turn up on the final walk-through.

✔ If something is found to be not working at the walk-through, you will have a chance to negotiate either having the problem corrected, repaired, or replaced.

✔ The seller can offer you a monetary credit or agree to accomplish the corrections immediately.

✔ The settlement agent should hold an amount in escrow that will cover the needed repairs or replacements.

✔ When the work has been completed to your satisfaction, any remaining funds will be forwarded to the seller.

484 Expect your agent to join you for both the home inspection and the final walk-through.

✔ Once you have an accepted contract, your agent should be involved in all aspects of the contract.

✔ Your agent should attend the home inspection to understand repairs, replacements, or reasons for additional inspections.

✔ Your agent should have *firsthand* knowledge of home inspection issues that could null and void your contract if they are not resolved to your acceptance.

✔ Your agent should accompany you for the final walk-through but you should do the actual checking of appliances, and other items.

485 Have confidence in the way your buyer agent will protect your confidential information.

✔ Real estate agents cannot share your confidential information with other agents or people.

✔ Under a buyer representation agreement, they have a fiduciary responsibility to you and cannot release confidential information to others without your permission.

✔ Types of confidential information may be financial (e.g., the highest price you will pay for a property) or personal (e.g., an impending divorce).

486 Tell your agent when you are telling them something that you wish to be kept confidential.

✔ The agent is not a mind reader. If you want the agent to pass along the word that you must have a new home right away because you are expecting triplets, you must say so. Otherwise, this information would be considered personal and confidential.

✔ Showing your eagerness to purchase a certain property might impress the sellers, but it might also give them the upper hand in negotiating.

487 Expect your agent to attend the closing on your home.

Mark's Stories

✔ Your transaction is not over until the contract has closed.

✔ Your agent represents you *through* closing under a buyer's representation agreement.

✔ The transaction service providers (lender, settlement agent) look to your agent for direction through closing.

488 Rely on your agent to answer questions and review the documents for you at the closing.

✔ Your agent cannot answer legal questions but based on experience can help you understand the process involved.

✔ Your agent may spot an error in the HUD-1 settlement sheet that you might have overlooked (e.g., payment for discount points on the loan being in the wrong column).

489 Express your appreciation for a job well done by your agent in one of the following ways:

✔ Write a letter of appreciation to their managing broker or company president.

✔ Refer friends, family, and business associates to them (the best reward).

✔ Send flowers, potted plant, or gift certificate.

490 What to do if your experience with your own agent has not been what you expected:

✔ Write the managing broker outlining specific situations where you thought that the agent did not fulfill the fiduciary agreement either ethically or professionally.

✔ Do not refer friends, family, or business associates; word-of-mouth advertising can also be a negative.

491   What to do if you feel that the agent holding an open house did not represent the property honestly.

✔ Contrary to other forms of sales, some "puffing" is allowed under license law in some states.

✔ Puffing is defined as nonfactual or extravagant statements that a reasonable person would recognize as such (e.g., "This house has the most marvelous view in the county!").

✔ Complain to your own agent requesting that a complaint be made to the other agent's managing broker if you feel that the agent has gone beyond puffing into misrepresentation.

492   Whenever you are in doubt about a statement or claim made by the listing agent or agent holding an open house, ask questions until you are satisfied.

✔ If your question requires further investigation, ask your own agent to find the answer.

✔ If the listing agent offers to provide further information for you, ask them to convey the answers through your buyer agent.

✔ Misrepresentation is when incorrect information is knowingly given with the intent to deceive.

493   If you are relocating to another city or state, ask your local agent to find you an agent in another state.

✔ Your agent may have personal knowledge of agents located in other areas.

✔ Many real estate companies are connected through a common referral system.

494   Do not be offended if your agent is to receive some compensation for referring you to another agent.

✔ This practice is common among real estate professionals.

✔ The rationale for making a referral payment is that the new agent did not have any effort or expense in procuring the new client.

✔ Your agent will not take a chance of referring you to an incompetent agent just to receive a small fee; your own agent's reputation is also on the line.

495   How to fire your agent.

✔ Unfortunately, relationships do not always work out.

✔ If you no longer wish to work with this agent, speak to the agent's managing broker.

✔ If you have a signed buyer brokerage agreement, the broker can assign you to a different agent.

496 If you wish to terminate your buyer brokerage agreement, you must talk to the broker.

✔ The buyer brokerage agreement is bilateral and cannot be arbitrarily terminated by either partner.

✔ The broker can assign you to another agent or agree to release you from the agreement.

✔ The termination must be agreed to in writing to order to protect you from any liability for the commission.

497 As you interview prospective agents, discuss how the agency law works in your state.

✔ Every state has its own legislation regarding the role of agency in real estate transactions.

✔ You are never forced to work with a buyer's agent, but in most states if you do not have an agreement with a buyer's agent, you are not represented in the transaction.

✔ All parties to a transaction must be treated honestly, regardless of brokerage relationships.

498 Have confidence in the educational background of your agent.

✔ State real estate boards or commissions license real estate salespersons and brokers; the specific number of required hours varies by state.

✔ Salespersons must take a minimum number of hours of prelicense education.

✔ Brokers must take a minimum number of additional hours in order to apply for a broker's license.

✔ Both salespersons and brokers must pass a state license test.

✔ All salespersons and brokers are required by state license law to take a set number of hours of continuing education to renew their license either annually, or biannually.

499 Learn what is meant by the term *licensee.*

✔ A licensee is one who holds a license from a government or other agency, which permits that person to participate in the buying, selling, leasing, or management of property within that state.

✔ All licensees must take continuing education hours prior to renewal of the license.

✔ All licensees must adhere to federal, state, and local Fair Housing laws.

✔ The granting authority may only revoke a real estate license.

500   You have the right to ask for proof of licensure from your agent.

✔ Real estate agents are not allowed to show or sell real estate if their license is inactive, revoked, or suspended.

✔ The validity of a license can also be obtained through the state regulatory agency.

501   Find out if your agent has been disciplined by the local professional regulators or had a complaint filed.

✔ Contact or visit the state Web site for the regulatory agency that handles real estate licensing.

✔ Contact the local Board of REALTORS® for license information.

✔ Contact the principal broker for whom the agent works.

502   Inquire as to the proper name for the regulatory body for real estate in your state.

✔ The regulatory body that advises and sets policies regarding real estate licenses and transaction procedures in many state is called the Real Estate Commission.

✔ In some states the regulatory body is referred to as the Real Estate Board.

✔ The real estate commissioner is a person appointed by the governor to implement and carry out laws enacted by the legislature that pertain to real estate.

503   Take notice of the difference in authority between a salesperson and a broker.

✔ A salesperson must be affiliated with a real estate broker for the purposes of performing acts or transactions regarding real estate.

✔ A broker is a person or other legal entity licensed to act independently in conducting a real estate brokerage business.

✔ An associate broker is one who has passed the broker's examination but chooses to remain under the supervision of a principal broker.

504   Learn what is meant by the designation of REALTOR®.

✔ An agent who is a licensed REALTOR® is a member of the National Association of REALTORS® (NAR) and is sworn to abide by the NAR Code of Ethics in addition to all federal, state, and local Fair Housing laws.

✔ REALTORS® are required to take additional Code of Ethics training every four years.

✔ Violations of the Code of Ethics are reviewed by the local association of REALTORS® and sanctions are issued where a violation is found.

505 Ask your agent to show you a copy of the Code of Ethics that the agent has sworn to follow.

✔ The REALTOR® Code of Ethics consists of articles that pertain to the REALTOR®'s relationship and actions with clients and customers, other real estate agents, and the general public.

✔ Many state licensing rules and regulations contain a section on ethics and standards of conduct.

506 Know your rights under the Fair Housing Act.

✔ The federal Fair Housing Act prohibits discrimination in the rental or sale of housing based on race, color, religion, national origin, sex, handicap, or familial status.

✔ Anyone who feels they have been discriminated against may file a complaint with the state regulatory agency, or the Department of Housing and Urban Development.

507 Know your rights under the Real Estate Settlement Procedures Act (RESPA).

✔ RESPA is a federal law that deals with procedures to be followed in certain types of real estate closings.

✔ RESPA requires any lender to provide you with a good faith estimate of all closing costs within three days from the time you make application for a mortgage loan.

✔ RESPA requires that the settlement agent use a HUD-1 Settlement sheet at closing that delineates all credits and debits for both seller and buyer.

✔ RESPA requires that you be given a Truth-in-Lending statement that discloses all costs of obtaining credit to make your home purchase.

508 Learn how the agency relationship between an agent and the client affects the fiduciary responsibility.

✔ An agent can work solely for the seller through a listing agreement, which creates an agency relationship.

✔ An agent can work solely for the buyer through a buyer representation agreement creating an agency relationship.

✔ An agent can work for both the seller and the buyer as a dual agent, with fiduciary responsibility for both clients.

509 Expect any agent that you consider working with to explain agency relationships to you at your earliest meeting.

✔ All states require disclosure of agency representation early in the transaction (i.e., obtaining specific information from the buyer as to his or her financial capacity, as to the property he or she wants to purchase, or other information that may be deemed confidential).

✔ In some states, either a buyer broker agreement or a disclosure of brokerage relationship should be signed before property is shown.

✔ In most states, if the prospective purchaser does not have a signed buyer broker agreement with the agent, the agent is assumed to represent the seller.

510 Beware of the agent who seems to be "on the fence" concerning his or her fiduciary relationship.

✔ This situation, called undisclosed dual agency, is essentially fraud.

✔ All agents have the obligation to disclose to all parties who they represent in the real estate transaction.

✔ Agency disclosure should be made at the onset of any real estate transaction.

511 Do not be misled by the term *fiduciary relationship*.

✔ The term *fiduciary relationship* is part of the common law of agency and indicates a relationship based on trust.

✔ In some states, statutory law with specific duties and responsibilities to clients and customers has replaced the common law of agency, which incorporates fiduciary responsibility.

512 Be able to differentiate between *agency relationship* and *brokerage relationship*.

✔ An agency relationship is created whenever one person (the principal) delegates to another person (the agent) the right to act on the principal's behalf.

✔ A brokerage relationship is created when both parties sign a brokerage agreement or contract.

✔ Listing agreements and buyer broker agreements establish a brokerage relationship.

513 Find out the proper terminology used in your state for an agent who will represent you in the transaction.

✔ The most common name is "Buyer Agent" but other names such as "Independent Contractor," "Transaction Broker," or "Transaction Facilitator" may be used.

✔ Be sure that you are to be given full representation, regardless of the state designation for your agent.

514 Learn what is meant by the term *listing agreement.*

✔ A listing agreement is a contract authorizing a broker to sell or lease real property on behalf of another.

✔ The listing agreement gives the agent the right to collect a commission if the property is sold through his or her efforts.

✔ The listing agreement will give the broker the authority to offer the property for sale or rent through the Multiple Listing Service.

✔ Because of the provisions of the listing agreement, your buyer agent is able to prepare an offer to purchase for you on any property listed in the MLS.

515 Don't put up with pushy agents calling you trying to secure your business.

✔ The "Do Not Call" law of 2003 prohibits real estate agents from cold calling consumers if they do not have a previous business relationship with them.

✔ The National Do-Not-Call (DNC) registry went into effect on October 1, 2003.

✔ Real estate brokers are required to check any calling lists against the DNC registry.

516 Watch out for "permission to be contacted" on sign-in forms in a public open house.

✔ The Do-Not-Call legislation limits calls from real estate agents (as well as any other type of sales) to persons with whom they have a prior relationship, or who have given permission to be called.

517 Understand how real estate agents are compensated.

✔ A real estate transaction involves the seller (and occasionally the buyer) compensating the agents through a commission.

✔ In the traditional model, the listing brokerage pays the cooperating (buyer's) broker a percentage of the contract price or a flat fee.

✔ The cooperating broker then divides his or her side (equally or unequally) with the sales agent.

✔ The percentage split with the broker varies according to the independent contractor agreement between the broker and the salesperson. Typically, an agent receives a higher split with consistent upward sales volume

For Example:

- A property sells and closes for $100,000. The seller pays a commission to his or her listing broker of 5% = $5,000.

- The listing broker pays a cooperating commission to the buyer's broker of 2.5% = $2,500.

- The listing broker pays a split of 65% of the listing side of the 2.5% to the listing agent: 2.5% = $2,500 $2,500 x .65% = $1,625.

- The buyer's broker pays his or her buyer's agent a commission split of 52% of their side: 2.5% = $2,500 $2,500 x 52% = $1,300

- The listing agent receives $1,625 in compensation from the broker. The buyer's agent receives $1,300 in compensation from the broker.

518 Look for the following when selecting your real estate agent:

✔ Knows when to talk and when to be silent

✔ Is experienced in overcoming objections

✔ Has good time management skills

✔ Possesses excellent negotiating techniques that can get you from contract to closing

✔ Has organizational skills to manage all of the information in your real estate transaction

✔ Prioritizes well

✔ Uses technology with confidence

✔ Has good communication skills

✔ Is a member of the local Board of REALTORS®and Multiple Listing Service

✔ Is physically able to show properties: climb stairs; stand for long periods of time

✔ Able to work evenings, weekends, and holidays

✔ Able to work long days that extend into evenings

✔ Remains calm when client or other transaction participant's emotions are heightened

✔ Skilled in exercising professional and ethical judgment to solve contractual or negotiation issues

✔ Skilled in reading documents such as real estate contracts, disclosures, and license laws

✔ Has contacts with transaction providers who will help make the entire transaction go smoothly for you.

519 Look for the following in your prospective agent's brokerage firm:

✔ Strong percentage of market share

✔ Ongoing technology training

✔ Ongoing negotiation and contract training

✔ Has national relocation affiliations

✔ Has market presence and name recognition

✔ Has a consistent marketing program for listings

✔ Charges clients a transaction fee

✔ Has company and office procedure manual that includes code of conduct

✔ Has no current license

✔ Has ethics, or arbitration complaints

520 Look for the following in your prospective agent's managing broker:

Mark's Stories

✔ Number of years' experience as managing broker

✔ Number of years in real estate practice

✔ Number of agents under his or her supervision

✔ Number of offices broker is responsible for

✔ Has good problem-solving skills

✔ Is a good listener

✔ Is less concerned with getting the deal done than eliminating potential legal issues that could arise after the transaction has closed

✔ Is available on weekends for agent questions

521 Learn what a *traditional* brokerage firm means.

✔ The traditional broker firm offers consumers full-service transactions.

✔ Traditional brokerage firms represent sellers and buyers in their market area and typically have relocation, mortgage, insurance, and title services available for their clients.

522 Learn what a *boutique* brokerage firm means.

✔ A brokerage firm positioned within a market area to appeal to a specific consumer or market profile (i.e., upper-bracket properties, specific developments, or historic properties).

✔ Generally, a boutique firm is small and limited to only a few agents.

523 Learn what is meant by an *auction* brokerage.

✔ An auction brokerage holds auctions for sellers to market properties to consumers or businesses.

✔ In most cases this type of firm is strictly for selling property at auction.

524 Learn what is meant by a *single agency* brokerage.

✔ Buyer representation only: The agency represents only buyers in its market area.

✔ Seller representation only: The agency represents only sellers in that market area.

525 Learn what is meant by a *builder/developer* brokerage.

✔ A builder/developer brokerage focuses on new construction or rehabilitation of existing properties.

✔ Typically, agents must register a client on the first visit together to the property or sales center.

526 Learn what is meant by a *commercial* brokerage.

✔ A commercial brokerage specializes in forms of commercial properties such as office buildings, shopping centers, multifamily buildings, and land for development, businesses, and businesses with real estate.

✔ Although the license is the same in most states for both residential and commercial brokers, the real estate practices are quite different.

527 Learn what a *discount* broker means.

✔ A discount broker charges a lower commission for listings or transaction services compared to brokerage competitors.

✔ Discounts appeal to cost-driven sellers.

✔ All brokerage firms can offer full service or limited services in exchange for a lower commission or fees.

528 Learn what is meant by *fee for service* brokerage.

✔ The fee for service broker offers a menu-based format where the consumer contracts for specific services that are part of the transaction process at a fixed rate of compensation.

✔ Example: Enter home in multiple listing services for a fee of $750. Host public open house for $100. Negotiate contract for $1,000.

529 Learn what is meant by a *for-sale-by-owner* brokerage.

✔ This type of brokerage offers real estate advertising programs directly to sellers selling their own property.

✔ Other options include conversion to a fee for service or full-service brokerage.

530 Learn what is meant by *Internet/e-commerce/virtual* brokerage.

✔ An Internet consumer-based brokerage provides the real estate sales agent with sales prospects from the brokerage Web site.

✔ Typically, the real estate sales agent works from a home office and reports to a regional managing broker.

531 Learn what is meant by an *independent* brokerage.

✔ The independent broker is one who is not affiliated with any other regional or national company.

✔ An independent company may have several branch offices but does not generally cover too large of a territory.

532 Learn what is meant by a *national* brokerage.

✔ A national brokerage provides national marketing and name recognition.

✔ This brokerage may operate numerous branch offices throughout the country.

533 Learn what is meant by *regional* brokerage.

✔ A regional brokerage is affiliated with a company that provides regional marketing and name recognition.

✔ The region is usually limited to several states.

534 Learn what is meant by a *time-share* brokerage.

✔ A time-share brokerage specializes in marketing specified time intervals in a property.

✔ A time-share purchase may be for a set week at the same property each year.

✔ Time-shares are also sold that provide the right to use a selection of properties for a set amount of time each year.

535 Learn what is meant by a *rural* brokerage.

✔ A rural brokerage specializes in ranches, farms, agricultural land, or surrounding communities.

✔ Although the real estate license is the same for agents, the practice of selling rural property entails many different aspects.

536 Learn what is meant by a *resort or vacation properties* brokerage.

✔ This type of brokerage markets to out-of-market consumers for second homes, vacation properties, or alternative seasonal properties.

✔ The firm may also work with traditional sales within the vacation or resort community.

Chapter 4
Mortgages: What You Need to Know

Unless you win the lottery or come into a big inheritance from a long-lost aunt, you will probably need a mortgage loan in order to purchase your new home. The following are need-to-know items.

537 Start planning for a mortgage loan before you start looking for a home.

✔ In today's market, sellers want to be sure that the prospective buyer has the financial capability to purchase the home.

✔ Realistic financial qualifying will indicate the appropriate price range for you.

538 Set a date by which you would like to be in your new home.

✔ New construction can take from six months to one year for completion.

✔ Contracts for resale houses usually call for 45 to 60 days to settlement.

539 Calculate a minimum of 30 days prior to starting the home search to begin the loan process.

✔ The initial lender approval may only take a few days but the overall process takes from 15 to 30 days. Allow time for any problems to be corrected.

540 Ask your real estate agent to recommend three lenders that they have worked with successfully.

✔ Lenders often specialize in particular types of loans (i.e., government loans, Fannie Mae/Freddie Mac conforming loans, "Jumbo" loans, "low-doc" loans). You want to find one that matches your needs.

541 Check with your friends who have either purchased or refinanced a home in the past three months and ask them how they would evaluate their loan officer.

✔ The same loan products are available from many different lenders. The style and personality of the loan officer is important. You want someone whom you will be comfortable with and can work with easily.

542   Contact at least three prospective lenders but do not try to talk to everyone in the mortgage loan business in your area.

✔ You may find hundreds of home mortgage lenders to choose from.

✔ Talking to too many lenders will only provide redundant information.

543   Set up an appointment at your convenience.

✔ Many loan officers will meet with you in your home.

✔ Make the appointment at a time and place where you are comfortable.

544   Save yourself time and trouble by collecting all the information you can before your first meeting with a loan officer. A checklist of items includes the following:

✔ Copy of last two years' tax returns, signed and with all schedules attached.

✔ Copy of last two years' W-2 form.

✔ Pay stubs covering the most recent month and showing year-to-date earnings.

✔ Two-year employment history including addresses and phone numbers. Any gaps of employment of one month or more needs to be addressed in writing.

✔ Three-month account statements for all liquid assets, with all pages included for checking/savings, mutual funds, CDs/money market, IRA/401(k), pension funds, stocks/bonds, and trust funds.

✔ Document the source and amounts of any gift funds.

✔ Fully executed sales contract and listing sheet for home being purchased.

✔ Fully executed sales contract and listing sheet for home being sold (if applicable).

✔ Most recent credit card statements.

✔ Name, address, and phone number of landlords for the past two years.

✔ Name, address, and account number for current mortgage holder (if applicable).

✔ Name and address of institution, account number, balance, and monthly payment for all other loans.

✔ Copy of divorce, separate maintenance, or child support agreement (if applicable).

✔ Check for application fee if requested by loan officer.

✔ Driver's license or other picture ID.

✔ Evidence of any additional income (i.e., child support payments (if court ordered), seasonal employment, government assistance, Social Security benefits, statements of stock dividends).

✔ Veteran's Certificate of Eligibility (if applicable).

545 Calculate your gross monthly income (GMI).

✔ GMI is your annual income before taxes divided by 12.

✔ Remember that if you are paid every two weeks, you will have 26 pay periods in the year.

546 Determine your own comfort level for a monthly mortgage payment before meeting with the loan officer.

✔ The loan officer will qualify you for what the lender considers you can afford as a monthly payment, usually roughly 33% of your gross monthly income. This amount will vary depending on the amount of long-term debt you are carrying.

547 Make a list of all of your current ongoing debt payments. See if any commitments could be paid off in the next six months.

✔ Long-term debt that can be paid off in less than 10 months may not count against your debt-to-income ratio, which is usually 38% of your gross monthly income.

✔ Debts that will be included in the debt ratio are car payments, credit card minimum payments, student loans, child support, and any type of financing agreement where you have agreed to pay a set amount monthly.

548 Take into account any extra monthly expenses that you have.

✔ Transportation, childcare, parental support, medical expenses, school expenses, sports equipment, ballet, piano or art lessons, and other such costs are not included as expenses when calculating your debt-to-income ratio for a loan.

549 Itemize all of your cash resources: checking account, savings account, IRA and 401(k) accounts, whole life insurance policies, certificates of deposit, money market accounts, and stocks and bonds.

✔ You may have cash resources in addition to what is currently in your bank accounts. IRA, 401(k), insurance policies, and stocks can often be borrowed against at a fairly low rate of interest. In some cases, the lender may not count these repayments as part of your debt ratio because you are actually paying back yourself.

✔ Decide how much of your cash assets you wish to invest in your new home. It is always a good idea to have a cash reserve adequate to cover your new mortgage payment for two or three months.

550 Consider whether you have a family member who would be willing to give you a gift of funds to be used for down payment or closing costs.

✔ Anyone may give another person up to $11,000 as a gift with no tax consequences to either the giver or the recipient. It must be a *gift*, with no requirement for repayment. The giver will be required to sign a statement to that effect.

✔ Two parents could theoretically gift both their daughter and her husband $11,000 each, resulting in a total of $44,000 in funds for down payment or closing.

551 Choose a reputable company.

✔ Beware of "Just Started Mortgage Co." When the real estate business is booming, new mortgage companies spring up almost daily.

✔ If you have any doubts about a company, check with your local Better Business Bureau, the Mortgage Banker Association, or the Association of Mortgage Brokers.

552 Remember that the interest rate charged on the loan is negotiable.

✔ Even though a going "market rate" will be quoted at any given time, the actual rate of interest charged is determined by the individual lender.

✔ Beware of rates that are much lower than you've been quoted by other lenders. Some lenders can surprise you the day before closing with additional costs you won't have the resources to pay for.

553 Be sure to ask for a total of lender fees charged by that company from each lender that you are considering.

✔ Lender fees are charged in several different categories such as application fee, loan origination fee, document preparation, and other miscellaneous charges.

✔ The Real Estate Settlement Procedures Act (RESPA) requires that the lender give you a Good Faith Estimate of all closing costs within three days from application, but if you are shopping for a lender, you need this information prior to choosing one lender with whom you will make an application.

554 Beware of the loan that is too good to be true!

Mark's Stories

✔ Anything that claims to be "too good to be true" usually is! The interest rate may be attractive but the lender charges could be two or three times higher than other lenders. The only fair way to compare is by comparing the annual percentage rate (APR).

555 Recognize the term APR and how it can be used.

✔ The annual percentage rate (APR) is calculated by adding the interest rate to be charged to any discount points and other required lender fees to determine the actual rate of interest the lender will receive.

✔ In most cases, the APR will be slightly higher than the quoted interest rate (i.e., 7% interest with APR of 7.5%). If the interest rate quotes is 6% but the APR is 8.5%, it should be a warning flag.

556 Compare the benefits of working with a mortgage broker or mortgage banker.

✔ A mortgage banker is one who originates mortgage loans and then either retains them in portfolio (stays with the lender) or sells them to investors.

✔ The mortgage banker is compensated for originating and servicing a loan. In many cases, the mortgage banker continues to service loans even after they are sold to outside investors.

✔ The advantage is that the mortgage banker is working with his own money and can make underwriting decisions more quickly.

✔ A mortgage broker is someone who brings borrowers and lenders together, originates the loan and then places it with an investor. The mortgage broker is compensated for "match-making" and does not continue to service the loan.

✔ The advantage is that a mortgage broker works with many investors and may have a larger menu of loan products to choose from.

557 Check with your credit union (if you have one) to see if they make first mortgage loans on houses.

✔ Credit unions are doing more and more home mortgage lending today.

✔ The interest may not be any lower than going "market rate," but the lender fees are often less.

✔ The advantage is that the credit union exists to assist its members. The disadvantage is that the selection of loan products may be limited.

558 Learn the role of each of the players in the mortgage loan process.

✔ The *loan officer* is your first point of contact. He or she will fill out the formal loan application, listing all of your assets and liabilities, discuss different loan products, and advise you on the most appropriate for your needs. The loan officer will then collect funds to cover a credit check and appraisal.

✔ From this point on, your main point of contact will usually be the *processor*. The processor verifies the information you have given by mailing out Verification of Employment and Verification of Deposit forms, orders the trimerge credit report from the three primary credit reporting agencies, and prepares the case file for the underwriter.

✔ The *appraiser* is a person licensed or certified by the state based on education, experience, and examination, hired by the lender to estimate the value of the property you wish to buy.

✔ The *underwriter* reviews the loan package, taking into consideration your assets, debts, income, and credit history plus reviews the property appraisal and loan-to-value ratio. The underwriter can then approve, approve with conditions, or reject the loan. A loan can be approved with a condition such as paying off a car loan, showing proof of gift status, or other action. An incomplete file will be placed in suspension. It is important that you respond quickly to any request for further information at this point; otherwise you risk delay and possible expiration of your locked-in interest rate.

✔ The last step is the *lender-closing department* where all of the documents required for settlement are prepared. The file is then forwarded to the designated settlement agent.

✔ The attorney, escrow or other *settlement agent* determines that all terms of the contract have been met, closes on both the loan and the conveyance of property.

559 Seek out a mortgage broker that is knowledgeable and has access to a variety of different loan products.

✔ Some lenders specialize in government (FHA and VA) loans.

✔ A portfolio lender is one that retains the loan in-house. This option is often good if you have credit or other problems with qualifying.

560 Select a loan officer that is experienced and gives you a feeling of confidence after your first meeting.

✔ Focus on an individual who offers to educate you to all parts of the mortgage loan process.

✔ Select a loan officer who is willing to take time to answer all of your questions.

✔ Value a loan officer who returns phone calls and e-mail promptly and is proactive.

561 If you have any doubts or reservations about the loan officer at your first meeting, get up and leave! There are plenty of others in town.

✔ Do not give the loan officer any money for a credit check, appraisal, or other fees until you are sure that you want to work with this person.

562

Be prepared to pay for both a credit check (approximately $65) and appraisal (approximately $350, depending on type of property) at the time of application.

✔ If multiple purchasers are involved, each will need a credit check.

✔ If a wife has retained her maiden name, two credit checks will be required.

✔ Sometimes the credit check and appraisal fees are combined into an application fee.

563

If you working with a mortgage broker, do not agree to pay additional lender fees (other than for credit check and appraisal) up front. The mortgage broker is paid by the investor where the loan is placed.

✔ Mortgage brokers receive a commission of .5% to 2% of the loan amount (average of 1.5%.)

564

Expect to answer many personal questions on the Uniform Residential Loan Application (known as Form 1003) regarding your assets and liabilities.

✔ You are only required to list enough assets to show that you can qualify to borrow enough money to purchase the home you are seeking. If you have multiple assets in properties, stocks, bonds, or cash reserves, you only have to list those with any debt outstanding on the asset.

✔ The loan officer will generally fill out the form as you provide the information.

565

Do not deliberately falsify any information on your loan application.

✔ Common mistakes regarding exact payoff figures or required minimum monthly payments can be corrected.

✔ All information will be verified through the trimerge credit report, and verification of employment and bank accounts.

566

Present yourself with as much stability in residence, employment, and debt repayment history as possible.

✔ If you do not have two years of residence in the same place, provide an explanation.

✔ A minimum of two years of employment is generally required. An exception can be if you were in college, or if you have changed jobs but remained in the same field (i.e., moved as computer technician from one company to another).

✔ If you do not have two years' history of debt payments, be prepared to offer alternative credit.

567 Be prepared to offer alternative credit if you do not have a two-year history of payments (i.e., no car loan, credit cards, or other fixed payments).

✔ Alternative credit can be any type of regular payments (e.g., rent, insurance premiums, childcare, utility bills, cell phone, or Internet access bills.

568 Do not be alarmed or offended when asked to sign an Authorization to Release Financial Information form.

✔ The lender will need this release to obtain the following information:

- Credit report
- Bank accounts
- Employment records
- Mortgage history
- Other loans or securities

✔ A Tax Information Authorization form may be requested in order to obtain a copy of your tax returns.

569 Be prepared to make a larger down payment, pay a higher interest rate, and anticipate additional paperwork if you are self-employed.

✔ Self-employed individuals have no unbiased person to verify their income.

✔ You will need to provide:

- Copy of past two years' business tax returns
- Audited financial statement
- Year-to-date profit and loss statement

570 If you are a recent graduate in a new job, come prepared to loan application with a copy of your resume, diploma, grade point average (if favorable), tax returns, and letter of employment.

✔ The lender will look favorably on occupations with definite potential of increased income in the next few years (i.e., doctor, computer analyst, upwardly mobile government position).

✔ If you are in a new job, but in the same field, a letter of employment and past two years' tax returns may be adequate.

571 If you are a recent graduate, consider having a co-signer on the mortgage.

✔ Parents are often willing to be a co-signer for a recent graduate. They must understand, however, that this will affect on their own credit standing.

✔ Whenever co-signers take on a mortgage loan, all of the assets and the liabilities of each party will be taken into consideration.

✔ The mortgage loan is a negotiable instrument containing an unconditional promise to pay a certain amount of money and all parties can be held liable for repayment.

572 Be cautious about co-signing a loan with anyone.

✔ Remember, if they default, you will be responsible for the amount due.

✔ This potential debt will show up on your own credit report and will affect your credit score and your own ability to finance a home or automobile.

✔ Ask to see a credit report of anyone asking you to be a co-signer. (There is a reason they need a co-signer.)

✔ Investigate thoroughly anyone who asks you to be a co-signer, including family members.

573 Discuss the possibility of having your parents fund the entire amount needed to buy a home.

✔ You can sign a promissory note in which you agree to repay the money borrowed over an agreed-upon period of time.

✔ For you to be able to deduct your mortgage interest for tax purposes you will need to have a mortgage or deed of trust (depends on where you live) drawn up and recorded against your property in favor of your parents. The deed of trust is the mortgage document for your property.

✔ You and your parents should consult an attorney as well as financial and tax advisors concerning all options in this tip.

574 Consider the option of having your parents loan you the money for a down payment, with the rest financed through a mortgage lender.

✔ This down payment amount will either have to be acknowledged as a gift or as additional debt.

✔ If the gift is 20% of the sales price, no additional down payment will be required from the borrower. If the gift is less than 20%, the borrower will probably be required to contribute somewhere between 3% and 5% of the sales price.

575 Consider a third option of you and your parents purchasing the property jointly.

✔ You and your parents will apply together for the mortgage loan. All assets and liabilities for all parties will be taken into consideration.

✔ The title will be held in both you and your parents' names.

✔ Your parents should understand that if you default on the loan they would be responsible for making the mortgage payments.

576 Consider a fourth option of having your parents purchase the home and lease it back to you.

✔ You will not receive any tax benefits from this option.

✔ This option may be good for providing housing for a student in lieu of paying room and board fees to the college or university.

✔ The parents retain full responsibility for the loan and the property.

577 Be sure to make a photocopy of every document or other piece of information that you give to the lender. Also include the date of submission on each copy.

✔ One of the major frustrations of obtaining a mortgage loan is being asked to submit the same information more than once. It will be much simpler if you have photocopies handy.

✔ Pay attention to the dates of original submission. Any substantial change in the information should be noted and corrected.

578 Pull your own credit report before meeting with a lender.

✔ This can be done with any, or all three, of the major credit reporting agencies for a nominal fee:

Experian	1-888-397-3742	http://www.experian.com
Equifax	1-800-685-1111	http://www.equifax.com
TransUnion	1-800-916-8800	http://www.transunion.com

✔ You can also pull a trimerge report from http://www.myfico.com.

✔ The report will indicate the areas that have affected your credit score and in some cases, will suggest ways to improve your score.

579 Contact any vendors that have submitted incorrect information to the credit reporting agency.

✔ Contacting the credit reporting agency will temporarily remove the item from the report but will not correct it.

✔ According to the Fair Credit Reporting Act, the vendor must respond within 30 days.

580 Learn the basics about credit scoring before making loan application.

✔ http://www.Myfico.com has a complete, easy-to-follow description of credit scoring and how it affects your application for a mortgage loan.

✔ Fair, Isaac Company (FICO) is the company that developed the scoring system.

✔ Your FICO score is a number that reflects your credit history and current credit status based on credit bureau history and public records.

✔ Credit mistakes that lower FICO scores:
  • Maximum credit limits utilized
  • Bankruptcies, foreclosures, judgments, liens
  • Too many credit cards
  • High amounts of unused credit
  • Excessive credit inquiries
  • Late payments
  • Unpaid accounts

581 Compare your credit score with the following chart. The following numbers are only guidelines; interpretations of credit scores vary from lender to lender.

✔ 800–850   = Excellent
✔ 700–800   = Great
✔ 650–700   = Okay
✔ 600–650   = Marginal
✔ 400–600   = Not good
✔ Under 400 = Help!

582 Study the percentages allotted for the different categories under FICO scoring to see where you may be the most vulnerable.

✔ Payment History   35%
✔ Amounts Owed   30%

✔ Length of Credit History   15%

✔ New Credit   10%

✔ Type of Credit   10%

583 Learn the difference in the three types of accounts typically used by creditors.

✔ Installment account: where you sign a contract to repay a fixed amount of credit in equal payments over a specified period of time (e.g., car loan, major appliances, suite of furniture).

✔ Revolving credit account: where you have the option of paying the outstanding balance in full or make a minimum payment each month (e.g., credit cards, gas companies, department stores).

✔ Open 30-day agreement: where you promise to pay the full balance owed each month (e.g., American Express, local business accounts).

584 Make a list of the credit cards you have at present by type, interest rate, balance due, available credit limit, and minimum monthly payment.

✔ Close out accounts that you do not use. (They still count against your score.)

✔ Decide whether you really need such high credit limits. (Lower limits will improve your score.)

585 Pay off the ones with the highest interest rate first.

✔ Department stores are usually much higher than VISA or MasterCard.

✔ Gasoline credit cards are usually higher than VISA or MasterCard.

586 Consolidate debt into two or three cards.

✔ Only do this if it can be done without maxing out a card. (Maxed out counts worse than too many cards.)

587 Expect to wait 18 to 24 months after a discharge of a bankruptcy before you will able to obtain a mortgage loan.

✔ Seek out a lender that has favorable underwriting parameters for persons who have filed for bankruptcy.

✔ Expect to pay a higher interest rate and additional lender fees if you have been through a bankruptcy.

588 Learn what is meant by "B," "C," or "D" paper or credit.

✔ Lenders categorize the mortgage loan (the "paper") as "A," "B," "C," or "D." An "A" loan is when the borrower is well qualified for the loan (i.e., has a good credit score, adequate income, and established pattern of payments).

✔ Investors who purchase packages of loans are most likely to purchase A paper.

✔ B, C, or D paper is when the borrower has serious credit problems. The lower the credit score and the higher the number of credit deficiencies, the credit ranking progresses from B to D. D credit is most likely someone with bankruptcy, judgments, or foreclosure and a very low credit score.

✔ The ranking of the borrower's credit represents the amount of risk that the borrower may default on the loan.

589 Understand that if you fall into the B/C/D credit category, you represent a higher risk to the lender.

✔ Lenders categorize borrowers credit based on their credit scores.

✔ If you have had a bankruptcy, been unemployed, self-employed a short period of time, have unpaid medical bills, or been late on making payments on home or auto loans, you may be considered B/C/D credit risk.

✔ You will pay a higher mortgage interest rate and possibly higher closing costs than if you were an A credit risk.

✔ The increased interest and costs for your B/C/D loan is an insurance premium for your level of credit risk to the lender.

590 If you are in the B/C/D credit category, look for a sub-prime lender who specializes or specifically targets B, C, and D paper loans.

✔ Because of the higher risk to the lender, the interest rate will be higher and a higher amount of down payment may be charged.

✔ Do not confuse "sub-prime lender" with "predatory lender." The market has a definite place for sub-prime lending for those with less than A credit.

591 Beware of the predatory lender!

✔ A predatory lender is one who misrepresents a borrower's credit, to place them in a mortgage interest rate category that is higher than their credit score indicates.

✔ Predatory lenders often prey upon the elderly, the less educated, and those who are not proficient in English.

✔ The predatory lender may offer a low rate of interest but the discount points and other fees will be very high.

592 Insist on receiving a Good Faith Estimate of all proposed closing costs and also a Truth-in-Lending statement that will disclose the APR if you suspect that you are talking to a predatory lender.

✔ The APR (annual percentage rate) generally runs anywhere from one-half to one full percentage point above the stated rate of interest. If it is more than that, check to see if you are being charged exorbitant lender fees.

✔ Under the Real Estate Settlement Procedures Act (RESPA), all lenders are required to provide you with the Good Faith Estimate and Truth-in-Lending forms within three days of application.

593 Study the following terms so that you will have a better understanding of what those involved in the mortgage loan process are talking about.

✔ *Mortgagee*: the party receiving the mortgage, the lender.

✔ *Mortgagor:* the party giving the mortgage, the borrower.

✔ *Mortgage*: document establishing property as security for the repayment of the mortgage loan debt.

✔ *Note:* a written promise to repay a debt.

✔ *Deed of trust:* document conveying legal title to a neutral third party to provide security for the mortgage loan debt. The choice of whether to provide collateral for the loan through a mortgage or a deed of trust depends on individual state law.

✔ *Default*: failure to carry out the terms of the contract; the most important term being the agreement to make regular payments.

✔ *Loan-to-value (LTV)*: percentage of what the lender will lend divided by the market value (e.g., property worth $200,000 with a LTV of 90% means that the lender will loan 90% of the value, or $180,000, and a down payment of 10%, or $20,000, will be required from the borrower.

✔ *Qualifying ratios*: the percentage of gross monthly income allowed by different loan programs.

  • Front-end ratio is the amount allowed for total housing expense.

  • Back-end ratio is the amount allowed for total debt.

  Example: Fannie Mae/Freddie Mac ratios are 28/36 or 33/38 for affordable loans. FHA ratios are 29/41.

✔ *Points*: each point is 1% of the loan amount. Lenders often charge a 1% loan origination fee. Additional points may be charged to discount (lower) the rate of interest.

✔ *Buy-down*: a cash payment to the lender that lowers the rate of interest; often used a marketing technique by new homebuilders.

  Example: Property selling for $200,000 with a 2-1 buy down. Interest rate for first year is 4%, second year 5%, and life of the loan 6%.

✔ *PITI*: usual components of a mortgage loan: principal, interest, taxes, and insurance. Payment is attributed first to principal, next to interest. Taxes and insurance are paid from an escrow account. Interest and taxes are tax deductible.

✔ *Principal:* the balance due on the amount originally borrowed.

✔ *Interest*: the amount charged by the lender for the use of the amount borrowed.

✔ *Conventional loan:* any mortgage loan that is now government insured or guaranteed.

✔ *Government loan*: FHA-insured or VA-guaranteed loans.

✔ *Conforming loan:* conforms to Fannie Mae/Freddie Mac guidelines.

✔ *Nonconforming loan*: does not conform to Fannie Mae/Freddie Mac guidelines.

✔ *Jumbo loan:* one that exceeds current Fannie Mae/Freddie Mac loan limits.

✔ *First mortgage (or Trust)*: the primary loan placed on the property.

✔ *Junior, or second mortgage (or Trust)*: secondary loan sometimes used in conjunction with first mortgage or one placed sometime after closing on first; such as a home equity loan.

✔ *Portfolio lender:* one who retains and continues to service the mortgage loans in-house.

✔ *Prepayment penalty:* a fee charged by the lender if you wish to pay off part or all of the balance due prior to the scheduled end of the term; penalty not allowed on any conforming or government loans; most often seen in jumbo loans and ARMs.

✔ *Negative amortization:* occurs whenever the monthly payment is not enough to cover the interest charges for that month with the additional amount being added to the principal balance; results in an increasing principal balance rather than a decreasing principal balance as occurs with a fully amortized loan.

594 Think twice before paying points to buy down your interest rate.

✔ The rule of thumb for payback on points is that you should be holding your loan for a minimum of six years to make it advantageous.

✔ Ask your mortgage broker to calculate the payments and payback figures both with and without points.

✔ Points are not refundable so if you sell your home before the payback on points kicks in, you will have lost money by paying points up front.

595 Study the following list of the most common types of mortgage loans to determine which one seems to best suit your needs.

✔ 30-year, fixed rate mortgage loan

- available as both conventional and government loans
- fully amortized loan where loan is paid in full at end of term

- principal and interest payment stay the same for 30 years (taxes and insurance may increase over time)
- most popular type of mortgage loan based on its stability and the value of money over a long period of time

Example: Historically, the value of a dollar decreases over time (e.g., the $1,200 spent on a mortgage payment today will represent a smaller portion of monthly income in the future).

✔ 15-year fixed rate mortgage loan
- same as 30-year except amortized over 15-year period
- a larger percentage of each monthly payment goes toward repayment of principal, which results in a smaller amount of interest paid than in a 30-year plan.
- may be a good option for someone who anticipates a major change in monthly income or expenses after 15 years (e.g., retirement, child entering college, etc).
- the monthly PITI payment is considerably larger

Example: monthly principal and interest payment for a $200,000 loan at 7% for a 30-year term is $1,300.60; for a 15-year term the payment is $1,797.66.

✔ Adjustable Rate Mortgage (ARM)
- also known as a variable rate mortgage (VRM)
- adjustment period can be 1, 3, 5, 7, and even 10 years
- interest rate is tied to an economic index that fluctuates with the market
- a convertible ARM provides an option to convert to a fixed rate mortgage at some time in the future, usually at slightly over market rate
- a hybrid ARM offers one rate for a fixed number of years, then switches to an annually adjusted rate

✔ Balloon mortgage loan
- a partially amortized loan
- payments calculated as if for a fully amortized loan for a set number of years
- at the end of the set number of years, the entire unpaid balance becomes due

✔ FHA (Federal Housing Administration) insured loan
- entire amount of loan is insured by FHA
- mortgage insurance premium (MIP) charged on all FHA loans
- qualifying ratios are 29/41, allowing for more long-term debt
- allows for compensating factors
- loan limits vary by geographic area
- borrower must contribute a total of 3% toward down payment/closing

✔ Graduated payment mortgage (GPM)
- interest rate is set for term of the loan but borrower is allowed to make smaller monthly payment for the first few years of the term
- the difference between what is actually paid, and what is due for each month is added on to the balance due
- results in negative amortization

✔ Interest-only loan (also called term loan or straight loan)
- payment is made for interest only, nothing toward principal
- best application is for short-term agreement
- total principal balance due at end of term
- no equity builds up with an interest-only loan

✔ Low/Doc or No/Doc loan
- little documentation is required to qualify
- borrower's word is taken with regard to income, assets, and liabilities
- larger down payment and higher rate of interest may be required
- lender may reserve right to review past tax returns

✔ VA (Department of Veterans Affairs) guaranteed loan
- top 25% of loan is guaranteed by VA
- uses one qualifying ratio of 41%, may be less for large family
- lender will loan four times the current VA Entitlement with no money down
- active duty, veterans, reservists, and national guard are eligible
- no mortgage insurance is required, but a funding fee must be paid

596 Do not be afraid of an adjustable rate mortgage. As long as you understand the worst-case scenario and are willing to take that risk, an ARM may be a good option for you, especially if you only plan to stay in the property for two or three years.

597 Learn how an ARM is calculated so you can intelligently discuss that option with your loan officer.

✔ The baseline for the ARM is an economic index such as
- U.S. Treasury bills or bonds
- Cost of Funds Index (COFI)
- London Interbank Offered Rate (LIBOR)
- other economic indicators that are regularly published
- once selected, the lender must continue to use the same index

✔ The lender then adds a margin of profit to the index (usually between 2% and 4%).

✔ The index plus the margin equals the note rate (interest rate) to be charged.

✔ Because the note rate is usually close to current market rate, the lender will set a lower initial rate for the first adjustment period of the loan.

✔ Typical adjustment periods for an ARM are 1, 3, 5, or 7 years.

✔ The note rate is recalculated every adjustment period, but you are protected from excessive increases in the rate by established caps shown as 2/6, or 1/5.

  • The first cap is the limit of increase of interest rate for each adjustment period.

  • The second cap is the limit of increase of interest rate for the life of the loan.

Example of worst-case scenario:		**Yr 1**	**Yr 2**	**Yr 3**	**Yr 4**	**Yr 5**
One-year ARM based on COFI index	3					
Lender margin (cannot ever change)	3					
Note rate (index plus margin)	6					
Initial rate	2	**2**	**4**	**6**	**8**	**8**

In most cases, the index will fluctuate (both up and down), but regardless of changes in the index, the interest rate can never exceed 8 (initial rate of 2 plus life-time cap of 6). If the index should drop, the interest rate will decrease based on the same 2/6 caps (e.g., index drops to 2 plus lender margin of 3 = 5 for note rate).

If interest rate is currently 8, it will only drop to 6).

598 Take the following precautions if you are considering an ARM loan:

✔ Clarify the exact adjustment period. (Some ARMS adjust every month!)

✔ Look for a consistently low index figure.

✔ Verify the exact margin the lender will use.

✔ Identify the caps that will be in place on your loan.

✔ Make sure there are no prepayment penalties for early payoff.

599 Ask a loan officer to give you the maximum loan limit for an FHA loan in your area, or look it up yourself under Maximum Loan Limits at http://www.HUD.gov.

✔ The maximum FHA loan is based on 95% of the median house price for a certain area but is governed by set limits for both standard and high-cost areas.

✔ If the maximum loan for your area suits your planning, you may want to consider an FHA loan. The ratios are 29/41, allowing for more debt.

600 Think you have lost your VA eligibility? Maybe not. Some of the most common misconceptions about VA loans are the following:

✔ VA eligibility runs out after a number of years. WRONG. You remain eligible for life and the amount of entitlement is frequently increased. Current entitlement is $60,000, meaning a lender will loan $240,000 with no-money down.

✔ VA eligibility can only be used once. WRONG. Unless you allowed someone to assume your original VA loan, you have your eligibility back and can use it again. In fact, you have the benefit of the higher entitlement figure. You will pay a higher funding fee for subsequent use.

✔ Once someone assumes your VA loan, you lose your eligibility forever. WRONG. Even if that loan is still in place you may have a partial eligibility, which is the difference between the entitlement amount that has been assumed and the entitlement amount in place today. Also, it is entirely possible that the person who assumed your loan years ago has either paid off the loan or refinanced with a conventional loan. Either way, your entitlement has been released and you can use it again.

601 Review the following additional list of types of mortgage loans to increase your general knowledge of mortgage loan products.

✔ *Affordable housing loan:* umbrella term used to cover various loan products targeted to first-time homebuyers.

✔ *Assumable loan:* existing mortgage loan that can be assumed by another person; most conventional loans are not assumable; government loans are assumable with qualification of the new person.

✔ *Bi-weekly mortgage:* one-half of the mortgage payment is paid every two weeks, resulting in one extra full payment toward principal each year.

✔ *Blanket mortgage:* mortgage secured by more than one piece of property.

✔ *Blended rate (or wraparound) mortgage:* refinancing plan that combines the interest rate on an existing mortgage loan with current interest rate for an additional amount of loan.

✔ *Bridge (or swing):* loan used to bridge the gap when someone is purchasing a new home before they have gone to settlement on their previous home.

✔ *Budget mortgage:* another name for a loan that included taxes and insurance along with the principal and interest payment (PITI).

✔ *Installment sale (also called a land contract):* usually a private agreement between a seller and buyer where title is not conveyed until all payments have been made.

✔ *Carry-back financing:* whenever a seller agrees to finance either the first or a second mortgage on the property.

✔ *Chattel mortgage:* a pledge of personal property to secure a note.

✔ *Construction loan:* short-term loan made during the construction of a house.

✔ *Home equity loan:* either a lump sum or a line of credit made against the equity in a home.

✔ *Open-end mortgage:* one where additional funds may be borrowed without changing other terms of the mortgage, typical for construction loans.

✔ *Package mortgage:* mortgage secured by a combination of real and personal property; often used for vacation property such as a cabin, beach condo, or ski chalet.

✔ *Portable mortgage:* new concept; mortgage loan can be carried with you from one property to another.

✔ *Purchase money mortgage:* any loan used to purchase the real property that serves as collateral but usually refers to seller-held financing.

✔ *Reverse mortgage:* special program for senior citizens (62 or older), which utilizes the equity in the seniors' home to provide additional income without having to sell their home.

✔ *Sub-prime loan:* loan with risk-based pricing for persons unable to qualify for prime conventional loans; typically has higher rate of interest; credit scoring and appraisal are critical.

602 Do not be misled into thinking that an assumable loan is the best way to buy a house.

✔ The difference between the amount that can be assumed and the sales price often requires more cash than you can readily afford.

✔ Only FHA loans originated before 1989 and VA loans originated before 1988 are freely assumable and will have low loan balances. Loans originated since that time require financial qualifying by the purchaser.

✔ Conventional loans are seldom assumable and will need lender approval.

✔ When interest rates are low you are usually better off obtaining a new loan.

603 If you have an assumable loan that a prospective purchaser of your home wishes to assume, make sure that you will be removed from any liability for the existing loan.

✔ FHA loans originated since 1989 will require that the purchaser qualify and the original borrower has no further liability.

✔ On a VA loan, the seller will want a Release of Liability, which requires that the purchaser qualify for the loan.

604 Proceed with caution if you are approached about buying into a special program that will help you reduce your mortgage term by half by making bi-weekly payments.

✔ Paying one-half of the mortgage payment every two weeks results in 13 full payments per year, with the 13th payment going all toward principal.

✔ The idea behind this program is fine. Making one-half of your mortgage payment every two weeks will indeed cut your mortgage term in half.

✔ The catch is that you do not need to pay someone extra dollars to accomplish this objective; you can easily do it yourself by paying an extra amount toward principal each month.

✔ Some lenders are offering this program today at no extra cost.

605 Be very cautious about entering into a 125% loan in which you are actually borrowing 25% more than the present value of the property you are purchasing. If you should have to sell the property in the first few years, you will find yourself "upside-down" in the mortgage, owing more on the mortgage than you can sell the house for.

606 Help out your elderly parents, other relatives, or friends by introducing them to the Reverse Annuity Mortgage (RAM), which can provide them with extra monthly income for life without having to sell their home.

✔ The basic concept of the RAM is to provide the elderly with extra income by making use of the equity that has built up over the years in the home.

✔ The amount received is based on your age (minimum 62) and the location and value of the property, which must be all or nearly paid off.

✔ No payments are made on the loan until the last surviving senior either dies, or no longer chooses to live in the property.

✔ The principal balance, accrued interest, and other fees become due at the time the property is sold.

✔ The funds may be drawn in a lump sum, regular monthly installments for life, or for a set number of years. A fourth option is to establish a line of credit.

✔ Both HUD/FHA and Fannie Mae have reverse mortgage programs in addition to those offered by individual lenders.

✔ Both seniors and family members should review reverse mortgage documents carefully, preferably with an attorney. The HUD/FHA program called Home Equity Conversion Mortgage requires a two-hour counseling session.

607 Don't be discouraged if you think you do not have enough cash to be able to afford to buy a home.

✔ Zero-money down loan programs are available today from many lenders.

✔ Special programs for teachers, police officers, firefighters, and hospital workers exist in many cities throughout the country that provide funds for down payment or closing costs.

✔ Depending on how "hot" the market is in your area, you may be able to receive financial assistance from the seller to help with your closing costs. (In a hot market where multiple offers may be made for every property for sale, the sellers will have little incentive to want to help you.)

✔ Conforming loans (those to be sold to Fannie Mae or Freddie Mac) allow the seller to contribute 3% of the sales price with 5% down (6% with 10% down); FHA allows sellers to contribute up to 6% of sale price and the VA has no limit on seller contribution.

608 If you are turned down by a mortgage lender due to your poor credit history, seek out a sub-prime lender.

✔ Interest rates are typically higher than for good credit risks but usually a rate can be negotiated.

✔ Acceptable risk profiles tend to vary from lender to lender.

✔ After your loan has "seasoned" (had a good track record for a few years), you can apply to refinance at more favorable terms.

609 In a slow market when properties are staying on the market for many months, look for a seller who has a mortgage that is nearly paid off and that is eager to sell. The seller may be willing to "take back the paper," in other words to take the place of the bank and provide you the financing you need to buy the home.

✔ Arguments for seller financing include:
- seller can charge more in interest than presently receiving in savings accounts
- seller will have a steady source of monthly income for years
- in case of default, the seller has the right to foreclose

✔ Objections sellers may have include:
- does not want to bothered with keeping track of payments
- worried about having to go through foreclosure process if necessary
- needs a large block of cash right away

✔ Counterarguments to objections include:
- payments can be handled through an attorney or escrow agent
- foreclosure can also be handled through attorney or escrow agent
- the mortgage can be divided into several notes that are negotiable instruments that can be sold at any time (although at a discount)

610 If you have found the house you want to buy but you need a few more months to get the cash together for down payment and closing costs, ask the seller to accept a lease-purchase contract.

✔ You will negotiate a regular offer to purchase contract including sales price and all other terms except financing with a delayed settlement date (six months to a year).

✔ You can move in after a walk-through inspection and will pay rent to the seller at an agreed-upon rate until you are ready to settle.

✔ The rent payment is usually slightly higher than the current market rate for your area but you will request the seller to give you a credit back at settlement.

✔ You will agree to obtain financing at least 30 days prior to the stated settlement date.

✔ During the time you are a "tenant" you will be responsible for all repairs.

✔ The lease-purchase idea works best with a property that is vacant where the seller does not need all of the cash immediately in order to purchase another home.

611 Learn who Fannie Mae and Freddie Mac are and why you should care!

✔ Fannie Mae and Freddie Mac are the primary players in the secondary market.

✔ The secondary market is where primary market lenders (banks, savings associations, credit unions) package their mortgage loans and sell them in order to obtain more funds for future mortgage loans.

✔ Because Fannie Mae/Freddie Mac is willing to purchase these packages of loans, they set specific qualifying guidelines to be followed on each loan.

✔ You should care because you will be asked to fit within these guidelines.

612 Be prepared to fit within these guidelines if you are hoping to receive a conventional conforming loan.

✔ Maximum loan limit is set each year; 2004 limit is $333,700 throughout the country.

✔ Qualifying ratios are 28/36 or 33/38 for Affordable Loan products. (Front-end ratio is for total PITI payment, back-end ratio for total debt including PITI.)

✔ Minimum down payment is 3% of sales price (sometimes even 0%).

✔ Private mortgage insurance is required with less than 20% down payment.

✔ Seller contribution is allowed up to 3% of sales price with 5% down, 6% of sales price with 10% down.

613 You may hear reference to Ginnie Mae or Sallie Mae as part of the secondary market. You do not need to be concerned with these two.

✔ Government National Mortgage Association (GNMA) is a government agency that sponsors a mortgage-backed securities program based on FHA and VA loans.

✔ Sallie Mae is the secondary market for student loans.

614 It is not likely that you will ever get a loan directly from HUD (Department of Housing and Urban Development) but it is a good idea to know a little about how it may affect your home buying.

✔ It is directly responsible for Federal Housing Administration (FHA) and you may quite possibly be seeking an FHA loan at some time.

✔ This department enforces Fair Housing and Real Estate Settlement Procedure Act (RESPA) laws.

✔ HUD maintains oversight of Fannie Mae and Freddie Mac policies.

✔ Through the Community Development Block Grant program (CDBG), it helps local communities meet their development needs.

✔ Administration of the Section 8 program of financial assistance for renters and more recently for Section 8 to homeownership participants takes place through HUD.

615 Understand the difference between a deed and a deed of trust.

✔ A deed is the legal document that conveys ownership of property (often referred to as the title) from one person to another. The deed is always recorded at the courthouse of the jurisdiction where the property is located.

✔ A deed of trust is a financing instrument that gives the power of sale in case of a default by the borrower to a trustee who will then sell the property on behalf of the lender (called the beneficiary). It is a nonjudicial foreclosure, meaning no court action is involved.

616 Understand the difference between being *prequalified* and *pre-approved*.

Mark's Stories

✔ Your own real estate agent, the home sellers and their agent will all want to know if you are a qualified buyer. Sellers are reluctant to take their home off the market unless they have a contract from someone that they feel will have no problem obtaining financing in order to settle on the property.

✔ You are in a much stronger bargaining position if you are pre-approved.

617 Expect to be prequalified by possibly your real estate agent, and certainly the loan officer, at the very beginning of the home-buying process. Even though you may consider these to be personal questions, do not be offended. Both the real estate agent and the loan officer need this information in order to do their best job for you.

✔ Real estate agents with a good grasp of finance may prequalify at your first meeting in order to establish an appropriate price range of homes for you to look at. (It's distressing to set your heart on a beautiful $300,000 home and then find out that you only qualify for a $150,000 loan.)

✔ The loan officer at your first meeting, or possibly over the phone, will ask a series of questions about your finances such as employment, income, debt, credit history, and funds for down payment and closing costs. From these questions an estimate can be made about the amount of a loan that you can afford. Computer technology today has made it possible for a loan officer to enter all of your information into a computer and receive an answer back regarding your qualification in minutes.

✔ Very little information is verified for a prequalification. It is simply a loan officer's estimate of the amount of a loan one can afford. The advantage is that it is quick and involves no cost and little effort. It will throw up a red flag if it encounters serious problems, giving you time to make corrections before making a formal application.

✔ A prequalification does not offer any commitment by the financial institution to extend credit.

618 Be able to recognize when *pre-approval* is in fact a *preapproval*, and when it is merely a *prequalification*.

✔ A preapproval involves actually applying for a specific mortgage loan even before a property has been selected and generally entails meeting with the loan officer in person.

✔ A loan application form is completed, a Good Faith Estimate of Closing Costs is reviewed,, and numerous disclosures are signed. Documentation such as pay stubs, W2s, tax returns, and bank statements are submitted. Information on the application such as employment, income, and money in the bank is verified.

✔ A detailed trimerge credit report is pulled for a review of credit history and to obtain credit score.

✔ An underwriter at the financial institution reviews this information and if approved, a written Letter of Commitment is issued.

✔ The commitment will be conditional pending an appraisal of the property selected for purchase.

✔ The Letter of Commitment will often read, "approved up to _____ [a specific amount of money.]."

619 Be patient. Although loan approval can occasionally be achieved in a matter of hours, two to five business days is more typical. If specific credit issues require explanation, the process could take 30 to 45 days.

620 Make sure that your Letter of Commitment includes all of the following terms and conditions: interest rate, term of the loan, lender fees, annual percentage rate, mortgage and hazard insurance requirements and any other special conditions imposed by the lender, such as prepayment penalties.

621   Expect to receive a Good Faith Estimate from the lender within three days of making a formal application. This estimate of all costs associated with settling on both a mortgage loan and property is required by law under Real Estate Settlement Practices Act (RESPA).

✔ Take the time to go over this form carefully. If you aren't sure why some fees are being charged or what they are for, ask your mortgage broker to explain them. Some of these fees are negotiable.

✔ When you are near the time for closing of your loan, you should be issued an updated Good Faith Estimate, which you should compare with your original estimate.

✔ Ask for an explanation of any large increases. Unreasonable, last minute charges can sometimes be waived at the closing table.

✔ Some of the charges shown are for past-through items that are being charged by outside third parties (e.g., survey, termite inspection, hazard insurance, and delivery fees). Other charges are either from the lender or closing attorney or escrow agent fees.

✔ A simple rule of thumb for closing costs is 3% to 4% percent of the sales price. If your charges are much less than that, it probably indicates some mistake. If they are much over that amount, ask for a detailed explanation.

622   Do not panic when you receive the original Truth-in-Lending statement within three days after your application. At first glance, it will appear that you are being charged a higher rate of interest than the one you were quoted.

✔ The Truth-in-Lending Act (TILA) is a federal statue that requires disclosure of specific loan information to the borrower before the obligation becomes effective.

✔ TILA applies to mortgage loans but also to all other types of extended credit.

✔ The premise is that the borrower should be able to compare the cost of a purchase if paid for in cash versus the costs when using credit.

✔ The act, though its Regulation Z, also covers how financing is advertised. If any part of the financing is mentioned, complete disclosure of all financing information is required which explains why you often see the tiny print at the bottom of an advertisement).

✔ The TILA statement will refer to your APR (annual percentage rate). This will most likely be higher than the rate that you have been quoted because it includes any points paid on the loan plus all other lender fees. If the APR is more than one full percentage point higher than the agreed-upon interest rate, demand an explanation. The lender may be charging excessive points or fees.

✔ Also included in the TILA statement are the total amount of finance charges for the duration of the loan, any prepayment penalties, late payment charges, and the amount actually provided by the lender at closing.

623 **If you love to work at your computer, you may want to try applying online for a mortgage. It is not as simple as ordering airline tickets but many people today have been pleased with this high-tech way to apply for a mortgage loan.**

Mark's Stories

✔ A big plus for online application is the rapid approval, streamlined process for highly qualified borrowers, and nondiscriminatory process. Some online lenders can respond to your application within 30 minutes.

✔ Online applications eliminate redundancies in the application process. Once you type in the loan application, the lender receives an electronic credit report for you and sends the information to their underwriters.

✔ A few negatives for online application include some factors that can't be addressed in an automated application could be the difference between approval and rejection. A promotion that is in the works, an inheritance that is through probate but not distributed, or the fact that your home expense will actually decrease if you purchase a home.

✔ Although many online lenders are completely reputable and provide good service, some have been known to throw in exorbitant charges at the last moment, fail to send the funds on time, and even to go bankrupt just prior to your scheduled settlement.

✔ If you have a lot of questions or it is the first time applying for a mortgage you might be more comfortable talking in person to a mortgage loan consultant.

624 **If you have good income but are short on cash you may want to consider one of the various no-money-down mortgages available today.**

✔ You should be prepared to still pay out-of-pocket costs associated with closing a loan such as application fee, appraisal, credit check, attorney or closing escrow fees, home insurance policy, home inspection fee, title search and insurance charges, recording fees, and miscellaneous closing costs.

✔ Most no-money-down loan products requires that the borrower have a very good credit score, because the risk to the lender is much higher without a down payment.

625 **Recognize the downside to no-money-down mortgages.**

✔ In some markets that experience no or small appreciation you may need to bring a check to closing if you decide to sell your home in the first five years because of a job or lifestyle change.

✔ You are building equity more slowly because a high percentage of your monthly payment goes to interest and not principal, especially in the first five years.

Example: $200,000 30-year loan at 7%, total P&I payment = $ 1,330.60
Payment #1: interest = $ 1,166.67, payment to principal = $ 163.93
payment #2: interest = $ 1,165.71, payment to principal = $ 164.89

626 Don't believe it if someone tells you that you can never obtain a mortgage loan because you have a judgment, bankruptcy, or foreclosure on your public records.

✔ The simplest way to remove a court-decreed judgment from your record is to pay it off. If it something that you dispute, try to resolve it as quickly as possible.

✔ If you have a bankruptcy on your record, the lender will want to know what caused it to happen. In cases of job loss, divorce, or catastrophic illness, the lender may be willing to work around this situation as long as the bankruptcy has been discharged for approximately two years. If the cause of the bankruptcy was 14 credit cards maxed out to the limit, it will take a lot longer before you will be eligible for a mortgage loan.

✔ Any lender will be wary of someone with a foreclosure on there record. They may reason that if you did it once, you might do it again. As in the case of a bankruptcy, the lender will want an explanation of why and how it happened.

✔ Because of the increased risk to the lender, you can expect to pay a higher rate of interest and possibly be required to make a larger down payment.

✔ If a conventional lender will not give you approval, work with a sub-prime lender. Their primary function is to help those with B, C, or D credit.

627 Take a pragmatic approach to the question of whether "to lock or not to lock" in the interest rate being offered. No one can second-guess whether mortgage interest rates will go up or down in the next few weeks. If you have been offered an interest rate that you are comfor-table with and you can afford, it is probably best to lock it in right away.

628 Be prepared to be charged mortgage insurance if you are making less than a 20% down payment.

Mark's Stories

✔ If the borrower has less than 20% down payment, the loan is submit-ted to a private mortgage guaranty insurer and you will be asked to pay monthly private mortgage insurance premiums, also known as PMI.

✔ The loan is usually submitted the same time the lender underwrites the loan. The underwriter at the mortgage guaranty insurance company reviews the loan package.

✔ If approved, the loan goes back to the closing department of the lending institution for closing and final packaging. Most loans are approved in 24 hours or less. If more information is needed to make a decision, the loan is put into suspense and additional information is requested from the lender.

✔ PMI premiums range from .5% to 1.5% of the loan amount, depending on the amount of down payment and also of the perceived credit risk of the borrower.

629 Make a note of the time when your PMI must be eliminated.

✔ Under the Homeowners Protection Act of 1998, mortgage lenders must cancel PMI insurance at the borrower's written request whenever the loan is paid down to 78 percent of the original value of the house. (Results in 22% equity.)

✔ You must be current in your mortgage payments and have no other loans on your home.

✔ It takes approximately 15 years to reach this point in your mortgage balance.

✔ The 1998 legislation does not take into account any appreciation of the value of the property. If your home is in an area of high appreciation, ask your lender if that will qualify for PMI cancellation. If it does qualify, have a full-time licensed residential property appraiser appraise your home under current market values and request that the PMI be dropped.

630 Talk with your lender about other ways to avoid paying for private mortgage insurance.

✔ Some lenders offer a lender-paid PMI program in which the interest rate is slightly higher but no PMI is charged. A benefit of this program is that the entire interest charge is tax deductible. (PMI insurance is not.) A downside of this program is that at no time in the future will the extra charge be dropped.

✔ Another way to avoid PMI is to keep the first mortgage at 80% of the sales price and add a second mortgage of 10% or 15%. The remaining 10% (or 5%) will be the down payment. The second mortgage is usually for a shorter term and at a higher rate of interest but the total monthly payment is actually a few dollars less than a 90% or 95% loan-to-value would be. This arrangement is called an 80-10-10 or 80-15-5.

Example: $200,000 sales price

160,000 first mortgage; 30 years at 7%

20,000 second mortgage: 15 years at 9%

20,000 down payment

631 Take time to learn what happens in the closing process now. When the big day arrives you will be too nervous to pay much attention to what is going on. The entire process becomes a big blur of papers being thrust at you for signature.

✔ After your loan is approved the lender's closing department coordinates with your selected settlement attorney or escrow agent who does the following:

  • prepares an abstract of title, which is a historical summary of all recorded documents affecting the title to the property

  • orders title insurance

  • orders a survey if required by the title company

- collects a copy of the homeowners insurance policy and termite inspection report (where applicable)
- prepares the deed conveying title to the property

✔ Duties performed by the escrow or closing agent at closing (or settlement) include:

- prepares the HUD-1 settlement statement required by law
- gathers proof of identity and photo ID from all parties to the contract
- finalizes all credits and debits for purchaser and seller such as tax and utility prorations, association dues, and condominium fees
- determines that all provisions of the purchase contract, including any contingencies, have been satisfactorily met
- resolves any issues arising from the final walk-through inspection
- performs all loan closing instructions by borrower's lender
- distributes loan proceeds (usually not done until all documents are recorded)

632 You will probably question whether you should purchase title insurance. The answer is "yes." This one-time charge protects you from anyone trying to make a claim on your property due to something that happened in the past such as a spouse that never signed off on a previous sale, missing heirs, an unpaid lien, or other defects that may not have shown up in the title search.

✔ You will have to pay for lender's title insurance to protect the lender's interest in the property.

✔ For a nominal amount you can obtain owner's title insurance that includes the lender protection plus protects you from any financial loss due to adverse claims to your title to the property.

✔ The title insurance policy is sent to you several weeks after closing. Be sure to keep it with your other closing documents.

633 Don't be confused by the interchangeable terms of *closing* and *settlement*. They both refer to the day when you *close* on your loan and *settle* on the purchase of your new property. Another confusion is over the words *in escrow*.

✔ In the western United States the closing is typically held in escrow where all parties sign their documents and entrust them to the escrow agent.

✔ In the East and Midwest either a real estate attorney or a title company agent conducts the closing. Usually all the parties to the real estate contract are present.

✔ In the East, the word *escrow* generally refers to the portion of the PITI payment that the lender collects each month in order to pay the next year's tax and insurance bills. These funds are called the *impound* account in the West.

634 Ask for quotes on homeowners insurance from at least three different sources.

✔ One obvious choice is the company that currently carries your car insurance.

✔ The lender will require you to have hazard insurance that covers the property in case of fire, flood, or other natural disaster.

✔ You will also want liability insurance that protects you in case someone becomes injured on your property.

✔ The combined hazard and liability policy is referred to as homeowners insurance.

✔ You will pay for one full year's policy at settlement. Then the lender will escrow one-twelfth of the next year's payment each month at part of the PITI payment.

635 Learn what rights you have as a consumer in the purchase of real estate and do not be afraid to insist on having them respected. Several government acts provide you with these rights including:

✔ *Fair Housing Act:* no one may be denied access to property for lease or for sale or for financing thereof based on their race, color, religion, national origin, sex, familial, or handicapped status.

✔ *Equal Credit Opportunity Act (ECOA):* protects you against discrimination from a lender based on race, color, religion, national origin, sex, marital status, age, or receipt of public assistance. Regulation B also states that you have a right to receive a copy of the appraisal, which you have paid for.

✔ *Real Estate Settlement Procedures Act (RESPA):* requires the lender to give you a Good Faith Estimate within three days of application plus an updated version at settlement. Also requires that a standard HUD-1 settlement statement be used.

✔ *Truth-in-Lending Act (TILA):* requires that you receive a disclosure of all costs of obtaining credit. Also mandates full disclosure of all financing in advertising.

636 Plan ahead in order to bring either a certified or cashier's check to settlement. The closing attorney or agent should be able to give you the exact figure the day before closing, but if it is not available, your real estate agent can calculate an estimate.

✔ If your check is for too much, the settlement agent will issue a refund.

✔ If your check is not enough, the settlement agent will accept a personal check.

✔ Do not bring thousands of dollars in cash to settlement!

✔ Pay attention to the date and time of closing in order to be able to get to the bank in plenty of time to obtain the certified or cashier's check. They do not usually issue these from the drive-thru window.

637 Do not be surprised if you are told that your loan has already been sold. Almost all residential loans are packaged and sold at some point, but occasionally this happens even prior to the official closing.

Mark's Stories

✔ Nothing about your loan changes except possibly the address where you send payment. All terms and conditions remain the same.

✔ Some lenders sell the loan but continue to service it. In this case, you may not even realize it has been sold.

✔ Do not take this event as a rejection, it is merely common business practice.

✔ If you receive a letter saying that your loan has been sold and you should now start making payments to a new company, be sure to verify with your original lender. Some unscrupulous companies work this scam.

638 If you are considering an FHA loan, you may want to learn more about something called a Green Mortgage.

✔ The U.S. Department of Housing and Urban Development offers the Energy Efficient Mortgages Program (EEM), which helps homebuyers or homeowners save money on utility bills by enabling them to finance the cost of adding energy-efficient features to new or existing housing as part of their FHA-insured home purchase or refinancing mortgage.

✔ Please see appendix for Web site information under Green Mortgages.

PART 2
Selling

Chapter 5
Getting Your Home Ready to Sell

639   Research how long your home could be on market.

✔ In 2003, the typical home sold in five weeks, one week longer than in 2001, down from eight weeks recorded for most of the 1990s.

Source: 2003 National Association of REALTORS® Profile of Home Buyers and Sellers

640   Learn how long the average homebuyer searches and the number of homes that can be seen.

✔ Weeks (median) 8
Homes seen (median) 10

Source: 2003 National Association of REALTORS® Profile of Home Buyers and Sellers

641   Research ways for you to realize the best obtainable price for your home.

✔ First impressions.

✔ Exterior.

✔ Interior.

✔ Appeal to the senses.

✔ Overlooked areas such as attics, basements, garages, and porches.

642   Develop a home enhancement plan before you place your home on market.

✔ Take an inventory room-by-room.

✔ View your home from a buyer's perspective.

✔ Invite friends or relatives over for a constructive evaluation.

✔ Attend public open houses in your community to gather ideas.

✔ Stand in front of your house and evaluate its curb appeal.

643 Establish that first impressions of your home will guide a buyer's reactions to it.

✔ Buyers will decide in very little time an opinion of your home.

✔ Buyers are critical of first impressions because they want friends and family who come to visit them if they purchase your home to have a favorable impression.

✔ Visit model homes in your community to see firsthand what the perfect first impressions can be.

644 Remember the exterior of your home or building is the first scene of your property the buyer will experience.

✔ Sweep and remove litter, leaves, and debris from street in front of your home.

✔ Remove weeds and edge sidewalks for a crisp look.

✔ Paint or purchase a new mailbox and entry light. Make sure light fixtures work and have active light bulbs.

✔ Lubricate storm and entry doors.

✔ Paint worn fencing and lubricate gates.

✔ Lawn should be weed free, healthy, and freshly mowed.

✔ Trim trees and bushes.

✔ Flowerbeds mulched and weeded.

✔ Blooming annuals add color.

✔ Decks and patios clean and stain-free.

✔ Walkway to front door weed-free and clean.

✔ Driveway clean and sealed.

✔ Repair cracks and potholes in driveway and sidewalks.

✔ Driveway should be free of cars, boats, and RVs.

✔ House exterior should appear well maintained.

✔ Add shutters or window boxes to warm up your home's street appearance.

✔ Replace broken windows.

✔ Clean windows inside and out.

645 Clean up all dog and other animal droppings before every showing.

✔ Droppings attract insects and pests.

✔ Buyers could walk in the yard.

✔ Presents a well-maintained look.

646 Recognize that buyers will pay extra attention to your roof.

✔ Replace all broken or missing shingles or tiles.

✔ Repair flashing in roof valleys or around chimneys and roof vents.

✔ Repair and paint eaves and fascia boards.

✔ Clean and repair all gutters and downspouts.

✔ All downspouts should direct water away from foundation.

647 Look for potential roofing red flags by buyers and home inspectors.

✔ Sagging roofs.

✔ Leaking roofs.

✔ Curling shingles.

648 Determine whether your roof is near the end of its useful life.

✔ Cracked, curled, or bare shingles.

✔ More than two existing layers of shingles will require tear off before new shingles can be installed.

✔ Replace old roofs before placing your home on market.

649 Have a complete chimney inspection on an older home.

✔ Tuck pointing of exterior chimney required.

✔ Flue, damper, and chimney cap in working condition.

✔ Ash pit cleaned.

✔ Chimney flue cleaned.

✔ Gas logs or starter cleaned and checked.

✔ Fireplace log grate properly sized.

650 Recognize that your front doorway should welcome buyers.

✔ Repaint the front door.

✔ Replace or install house numbers.

✔ Install new door hardware.

✔ Place outdoor flowerpot with flowers or seasonal greenery.

651 Consider having your siding, decks, and patios power washed before placing your home on market.

✔ Replace missing siding and trim.

✔ Remove moss from north facing siding and decks.

652 Eliminate these sound and smell first impressions or distractions from your home during home showings.

✔ Pet, smoking, or cooking odors.

✔ Noisy children or barking dogs.

✔ Loud music or televisions.

✔ Dishwashers and washing machines in use.

653 Be aware of personal statements you make in your home that could alienate buyers.

✔ Strong political or religious artifacts.

✔ Unusual art or furnishings.

✔ Sexually explicit materials.

654 Minimize personal and family photos.

✔ Buyers should be focused on your home and not your family or friends.

✔ Photos can share information with buyers about yourself that they don't need to know.

655 Decide how you will create the best first impression in your entry or foyer.

✔ Remove wallpaper.

✔ Paint neutral color.

✔ Remove clutter and streamline furniture.

✔ Clean floors, door hardware, light fixtures, and switch plates.

✔ Create an area for listing sheets and other property information.

✔ Have sufficient lighting accessible for evening showings.

656 Plan ahead if you want buyers to take shoes off when viewing your home.

✔ Have a feature card in entry asking buyers and agents to remove shoes.

✔ Some buyers don't like to remove shoes, have a wicker basket of surgical booties available for buyers to slip over their shoes.

657 Consider that most buyers don't utilize living rooms but want them to make statement.

✔ Keep drapes and blinds clean and in working condition.

✔ Clean, polish, or refinish hardwood floors.

✔ Dust and clean furniture.

✔ Arrange furniture to best complement room.

✔ Replace, repair, or upgrade lighting.

✔ Have area rugs or carpeting professionally cleaned.

✔ Replace worn or dated carpeting.

✔ Clean windowsills, shutters, and doors.

✔ Eliminate ceiling water stains, cracks, or peeling paint.

658 Plan ahead to make a special effort on your kitchen because it is the most important room to buyers.

✔ Outdated appliance colors should be professionally refinished in almond or white.

✔ Spruce up kitchen cabinets with new hardware and knobs.

✔ If cabinets are old, or in poor condition have them updated with new fronts.

✔ Clean the exterior of all appliances including the disposal.

✔ Clean the top of the refrigerator.

✔ Clean dead bugs out of light fixtures.

✔ Dust high ledges and shelves.

✔ Check that all functions on all appliances work.

✔ Replace chipped, cracked, or outdated countertops.

✔ Clean all tile grout.

✔ Re-caulk kitchen sink.

✔ Check for leaks in kitchen plumbing.

✔ Organize your kitchen cabinets, dispose of out-dated products. Group like kinds together.

✔ Replace worn floors.

✔ A good paint job will zip up your kitchen.

659 Plan ahead to replace old appliances.

✔ New appliances can add a quick update to a tired kitchen.

✔ Buyers will subtract more than the actual replacement cost from list price for old appliances.

660 Clean the interiors of all kitchen appliances.

✔ Refrigerator.

✔ Stoves/ovens.

✔ Trash compactor.

✔ Dishwasher.

✔ Wine/bar refrigerators.

✔ Microwaves.

661 Clear all countertops off of all but the bare essentials.

✔ You'll be amazed at how big your kitchen looks.

✔ Cluttered countertops add years to the look of your kitchen.

662 Recognize that your bathrooms will come under scrutiny by home shoppers.

✔ Replace your toilet seat.

✔ Store all personal care items out of sight.

✔ Install towel racks to update an old bathroom. Have enough towel racks.

✔ Coordinating towels and shower curtains can unify a bathroom economically.

✔ Mirrors with peeling surfaces should be replaced.

✔ Scrub the tub and tile and eliminate all molds.

✔ Run exhaust fans at least 20 minutes after showering.

✔ Use room fresheners and colored bowl cleaners sparingly.

✔ Have tissues and toilet paper stocked at all showings.

✔ Empty wastebasket before showings.

✔ Clean shower curtain liners.

✔ Buyers want to feel clean and fresh in bathrooms.

✔ Make sure all faucets shut off completely.

✔ Make sure all drains flow freely.

✔ Clean shower doors.

✔ Caulk tub and showers if necessary.

663 Study home design magazines to help create a welcoming bedroom for buyers.

✔ Clean bedspreads, bed skirts, and sheets.

✔ Clean windows and mirrors.

✔ Have adequate lighting for evening showings.

✔ Organize closets so you can see the ceiling and parts of back closet wall.

✔ Don't cover the closet floor with piles of shoes.

✔ Bedrooms should comfort buyers.

664 Determine which overall home packaging ideas apply to rooms in your home.

✔ Streamline furniture.

✔ Furniture should serve function for room, no sofas in dining room.

✔ Create empty space near windows so buyers can see views.

✔ Compensate for tall buyers by adjusting ceiling fan heights.

✔ Draperies and blinds should complement room.

✔ Thin large artwork groupings.

✔ Have blank areas on walls in every room.

✔ Clean TVs and remote controls.

✔ Locate cable, DSL, and telephone connections.

✔ Minimize wallpaper.

✔ Repair nail holes from old artwork.

✔ Clean cobwebs from ceilings and walls.

✔ Have appropriate lighting for evening showings.

✔ Remove valuables or fragile items.

665 Decide how you can put the best face on your basement.

✔ Paint the stairs to the basement.

✔ Paint your basement floor.

✔ Make sure your basement is well lit.

✔ Clean, organize, and streamline your basement.

✔ Clean and organize your laundry area.

✔ Do not leave undergarments or other laundry on clotheslines during showings.

✔ Put away clotheslines so that buyers don't get hung up on them.

✔ Leave no signs of pest infestation.

✔ Eliminate dampness with a dehumidifier.

✔ Clean the boiler, hot water heater, and water softener.

✔ Clear an area in front of the electric panel, furnace, water heater, and sump pump.

✔ Clean all animal smells.

✔ Wash basement windows.

✔ Eliminate water seepage in basement.

✔ Pour water and bleach into floor drains to freshen.

✔ Paint walls white to lighten dark spaces.

✔ Remove rusty cabinets and bookshelves.

✔ Determine whether water stains on walls are new or old, if old paint with stain killing paint.

✔ Find alternatives to mothballs.

✔ Sweep outside basement stairwells.

666 Look for ways to make your garage more appealing.

✔ Clean oil stains from floor.

✔ Paint garage floor.

✔ Install automatic garage door openers.

✔ Organize garden tools, hoses, and holiday decorations.

✔ Hang bicycles.

✔ Use plastic totes for toys.

✔ Add additional lighting for night showings.

✔ Clean windows and doors.

✔ Remove cobwebs and animal droppings.

✔ Clean garbage cans to eliminate smells.

667 Study how you can make a swimming pool or spa more inviting.

✔ Repair or replace broken tiles.

✔ Repair cracked concrete.

✔ Pool and surrounding area should be clean.

✔ Pool landscaping should be trimmed.

✔ Position outdoor furniture to create focal point.

✔ Have life saving equipment visible.

✔ Night lighting adds drama to pools and spas.

✔ Replace worn pool equipment such as brushes, hoses, sweeps, pool covers, and nets.

✔ If pool surfaces are stained have cleaned or painted.

668 Realize that in some markets swimming pools could be a negative for buyers.

✔ Short pools seasons, June 1–September 1.

✔ Families with small children.

✔ Buyers who don't swim.

✔ Buyer's perspective of high maintenance time and costs.

✔ Other needs or uses for yard space taken up by pool.

✔ Liability issues.

669 Find out how much it will cost to remove a pool and return to yard in markets where they are more of a negative than a plus to buyers.

670 Anticipate that there will always be a minimum of three people congregating at principal points on a home showing.

✔ Make space available in each room for the buyers and their agent to stop and take a room in.

✔ Create a flow through your home to guide buyers from one stopping point to another.

✔ Barriers created by furniture arrangements, toys or pets will alter the natural flow of a home.

671 Effective model homes focus on creating the right environment.

✔ Neutral environment, so buyers can overlay their furnishings and lifestyle.

✔ Clean, fresh, and new smell.

✔ Attention to detail, with clean rooms, walls, and floors. Landscaping trimmed.

✔ Subtle background music, classical, light jazz, or rock on low volume.

✔ Interior décor and wall colors accent the home's architectural features.

✔ Live plants or fresh flowers add finishing touches.

672 Understand decorating basics that can guide you to repositioning a room.

✔ Color. A little goes a long way.

✔ Scale. Do furniture sizes complement or overwhelm a room?

- ✔ Pattern. Easy does it to avoid distracting from room itself.
- ✔ Lighting. Use it to brighten and illuminate dark corners. Helps to fill out a room.
- ✔ Focal point. Fireplaces, artwork, architectural elements that a room can be built around. Every room needs one.
- ✔ Furniture arrangement. Functional and room-enhancing to feature your home at its best.
- ✔ Texture. Adds visual interest and can warm up cold spaces and finishes.

673 Have floor plans of your home available for buyers to take with them and overlay their furniture.

- ✔ Room dimensions.
- ✔ Door and window openings.
- ✔ Wall lengths for furniture placement.
- ✔ Sun and light exposure directions.

674 Study ways for your property to show well when you must move out while it is on market.

- ✔ Smaller spaces can appear larger empty.
- ✔ Leave some larger pieces to give rooms a scale: master bedroom bed, sofa in living or family room.
- ✔ Clean home thoroughly after you move out.
- ✔ Leave supply of cleaning supplies, toilet paper, and lightbulbs.
- ✔ Post photos in each room showing how it looked with your furniture.
- ✔ Rent furniture for major rooms.
- ✔ Vacant homes say "motivated" to buyers.

675 Consider these sure fire ways to kill a home showing.

- ✔ Troublesome locks.
- ✔ Offensive odors.
- ✔ Dirty dishes on kitchen counters.
- ✔ Unflushed toilets.
- ✔ Moldy bathrooms.
- ✔ Piles on dirty laundry on floor.
- ✔ Dark, creepy basements.
- ✔ Locked and closed bedroom doors.
- ✔ Distracting children or pets.

✔ Unmade beds, or bare beds.

✔ Liquor bottles scattered around home.

✔ Rodents or pests seen.

✔ All curtains or blinds drawn in home.

676 Discover negative nonverbal signals from buyers during a showing.

✔ Don't see the entire home.

✔ Don't touch anything.

✔ Leave within 5 minutes.

✔ Have no comments.

✔ Have arms folded.

✔ Nonstop sneezing or runny eyes.

677 Look for positive nonverbal signals from buyers during a showing.

✔ Revisit each room after initial tour of home.

✔ Smile or look happy.

✔ Take photos.

✔ Measure rooms for furniture.

✔ Sit down and take the home in.

✔ Remove jackets.

678 Decide how to set priorities when you are short of time to prepare your home. Most important to least.

✔ Paint interior.

✔ Paint exterior.

✔ Professional cleaning.

✔ Repair roof.

✔ Waterproof basement.

✔ Beautify bathrooms.

✔ New carpeting.

✔ Refinish hardwood floors.

✔ New kitchen floors.

✔ New furnace.

✔ Landscaping.

✔ Blacktop driveway.

679
Read the most popular upgrades by buyers of new construction according to the National Association of Home Builders.

✔ Flooring.

✔ Cabinets.

✔ Appliances.

✔ Carpet.

✔ Plumbing.

✔ Lighting.

✔ Counters.

✔ Electrical.

✔ Fireplace.

✔ Brick.

680
Consider the most popular options by buyers of new construction according to the National Association of Home Builders.

✔ Fireplace.

✔ Windows.

✔ Air-conditioning.

✔ Finished basements.

✔ Decks.

✔ Garage.

✔ Appliances.

✔ Additional room.

✔ Security systems.

✔ Whirlpool tub.

681
Research how to "stage" your home to maximize its appeal to homebuyers.

✔ Create a spacious and pleasant home environment for buyers.

✔ Start by removing the first thing that gets in your way.

✔ Take one or two major pieces of furniture out of every room to make it more spacious.

✔ Keep matching furniture pieces together to build uniformity in a room.

✔ Create seating areas where two or more people can talk.

682 Keep the eye moving when staging a room.

✔ Use furniture placement to direct the buyer's eye toward a room's features.

✔ Move large pieces of furniture away from windows.

✔ Place large furniture at entry end of room to lighten visual load at opposite end of room.

✔ Use area rugs to anchor seating arrangements.

✔ Have your dining room table closed to its smallest size.

683 Use furniture placed on angles in a room to give it a quick update.

✔ Angle a bed in a corner of a bedroom to focus attention.

✔ Angle furniture in a "V" shape in living and family rooms.

✔ If short on furniture in a room, angles can help fill in a room and lend a designer look.

684 Create vignettes in rooms to set a mood.

✔ Breakfast tray with coffee cups, newspaper, flower vase on bed.

✔ Set the dining room table with linen tablecloth, china, silverware, and stemware.

✔ Set up game table for chess, bridge, or backgammon.

685 Research quick and easy ways to zip up your home for a showing.

✔ Place bowls of potpourri around the home.

✔ Buy a new front door mat to welcome buyers.

✔ Buy new pillows for sofas.

✔ Make a centerpiece for dining or kitchen tables from fresh fruit or silk flowers.

✔ Place bud vases with cut flowers in bathrooms and on beside tables.

✔ Put a seasonal wreath on your front door.

686 Consider appropriate staging during holiday seasons.

✔ Understand not all have the same appreciation for all holidays.

✔ Keep decorations on the conservative side.

✔ Keep holiday music classical.

✔ Leave holiday treats for home buyers.

687 Locate through your real estate agent professionals who specializes in staging homes for sale if you don't have the knack or time.

688 Remember now is the perfect time to start thinning closets, cabinets, furniture, basements, attics, and garages of items you won't be moving.

✔ Donate to charitable organizations for tax deductions.

✔ Hold a yard or garage sale.

✔ Give to family or friends.

689 Recognize how to organize items that you don't need or want.

✔ Donate.

✔ Keep.

✔ Throw away.

690 Be realistic when deciding what to keep. Some sellers create piles each time they organize items.

✔ Create a go-back-to pile to help keep you moving.

✔ If you can't part with items, place them in a pile for a second round of decisions.

✔ Decide that you will part with 25% of a pile each time you go through it until it is streamlined to what you want to move.

691 Keep in mind a place in your new home for each item you want to keep.

692 Follow the one-year rule when determining how to organize an item.

✔ If you haven't worn a piece of clothing or used the item in one year, it is most likely something that you won't use in the next year. Is it worth the cost to move it?

693 Move items that you have decided to take to your new home but don't have a place for now to an off-site location while your home is on market.

✔ Self-storage locker.

✔ Family or friends' homes.

694 Remember not to shift storage items from one location to another in your home as you streamline.

✔ Homes with piles of boxes or stuffed closets and cabinets appear to buyers as not having adequate storage space.

Chapter 6

For Sale by Owner

695 **Consider selling your home without a real estate agent.**

✔ Known as For Sale By Owner, or FIS-BO.

696 **Locate three real estate agents to prepare a market analysis of your property even if you don't plan on listing your home with a real estate brokerage.**

✔ Use three different brokerages.

✔ Require full-time agents with a minimum of three years' experience.

✔ Respect their price opinions; they are in your real estate market every day.

✔ Remember that these agents, if you are willing to compensate buyer's agents, could have a buyer for your property.

✔ Resist listing your property if an agent says they will only show your property to their buyer if you list your home with them. Your home might not appeal to their buyer.

✔ Obtain a written market analysis that will compare a minimum of three comparable properties to yours that have closed, are under contract, or are active (competition).

✔ A comparable property will be of the same age, condition, style and features, and number of rooms, bedrooms, and baths.

697 **Become familiar with the top mistakes sellers make when selling by owner.**

✔ Overpricing their home.

✔ Not being available to show property.

✔ Allowing for no or low marketing budget.

✔ Not preparing their home for market (see Chapter 5).

698 Be aware of the dangers of an overpriced property.

✔ Diminishes "new inventory" excitement level.

✔ As market time increases, home becomes "stale."

✔ Longer market times often result in a lower selling price.

✔ Price can't be justified by an appraisal for financing by a ready, willing, and able buyer.

✔ Ultimately, buyer or market value will determine the selling value of your home.

699 Consider what affects the value of your home.

✔ Location.

✔ Competition.

✔ Timing.

✔ Condition.

700 Determine how your property location will impact buyers.

✔ Advantages: quality of school district; walk to transportation, schools, and shops; pleasant, quiet neighborhood; low crime rates.

✔ Disadvantages; busy street; near train tracks, high voltage power lines, and commercial buildings; across from hospitals or schools; airport landing paths.

701 Check out the competition for your home.

✔ Drive all streets twice a week in your neighborhood watch for sale signs, moving trucks, and contractors.

✔ Check newspaper ads.

✔ Do a search on http://www.Realtor.com weekly.

✔ Attend open houses of all new inventory that is direct competition for your home.

702 Consider the effect of time and activity when you first place your home on the market.

✔ The majority of your home's showings occur when your property first comes on the market.

✔ New inventory attracts the attention of the largest number of buyers looking for a home in that price range.

✔ The first two to three weeks on market will bring the most buyer interest and activity to your home

703 Consider a study completed by the National Association of REALTORS® of home buyers and sellers in 2003 asking where buyers came from.

✔ Real estate professional 86%

✔ Yard signs 69%

✔ Internet 65%

✔ Newspaper advertising 49%

✔ Open houses 48%

✔ Builders 37%

✔ Home book/magazine 35%

✔ Television 22%

✔ Relocation Company 14%

704 Remember after real estate professionals, yard signs attract the most buyers to a property.

✔ Select bold colors such as yellow, red, blue, or orange.

✔ If you have a corner lot, have two signs.

✔ Include your phone number and home Web site address if applicable.

✔ If your property is a condominium, cooperative, or in a homeowners association, check with the property manager to verify that you can place a sign in the yard or your unit's window.

✔ Have "shown by appointment only" on your sign.

705 Consider having a Web site for your property.

✔ A simple 1–4 page Web site with property information and photographs will provide buyers 24/7 access.

✔ Cost is $100 at http://www.networksolutions.com.

✔ Remember to have your Web site seeded in major search engines such as Google and Yahoo!

706 Learn how to write effective real estate ads.

✔ Review current real estate ads in your newspaper.

✔ Newspaper ads should contain at the minimum: a headline, property address, and price, number of rooms, bedrooms, and baths, contact information that includes phone number and Web site address for property.

✔ Develop several headlines for your ad that will draw attention to your ad. Bright Open Floor Plan! Move-In & Enjoy! New Kitchen & Bath! First Floor Family Room! Best of Old & New! Walk to Train & Shops! Open House Sunday May 1st!

707 Plan ahead for your public open houses.

✔ Use "Open House" and date as headline for your property ad.

✔ Have a supply of property feature sheets and hand to buyers as they arrive.

✔ Be open a minimum of two hours.

✔ Check local events calendars for potential conflicts for your open house.

✔ Have a guest registry.

✔ Clean, clean, clean.

✔ Rake leaves, mow lawn, or shovel snow.

✔ Pick up dog droppings.

✔ Move cars out of driveway.

✔ Eliminate pet and smoke odors.

✔ Turn on lights.

✔ Open blinds, shades, and drapes.

✔ Offer bottled water and cookies.

✔ Promote open house on property Web site.

✔ Place additional sign on yard sign "Open Sunday."

✔ Be friendly but not overbearing.

✔ Give buyers time to talk among themselves.

708 Developing a property listing or feature sheet.

✔ Top of page: property address, house number, street name, city, state, and ZIP code.

✔ Headline: Vintage Perfection! Charming Georgian! Custom New Construction! First Floor Family Room Overlooking Terrace and Gardens!

✔ List price of home: $259,000.

✔ List room, bedroom, and bath count: 8 Rooms, 4 Bedrooms, 2 Baths.

✔ Exterior photo.

✔ Year built.

✔ Most recent property tax amount and year: $3,689.14, 2003.

✔ County.

✔ Township.

✔ Elementary, middle, and high school names and district numbers.

✔ Assessment if condo or co-op.

✔ Room sizes for all rooms except bathrooms. Living room: 20 x 12, Dining room: 12 x 12, Kitchen 18 x 10, Family Room: 18 x 12, Master Bedroom: 16 x 14, Bedroom 2: 12 x 14, Bedroom 3: 12 x 10, Bedroom 4: 10 x 09.

✔ Type of heat: Electric, gas, hot water, oil, solar, wood.

✔ Air-conditioning: Central, window units #, evaporator.

✔ Fireplaces or wood stoves: Number, location, gas starter/logs.

✔ Exterior: Brick, vinyl, cedar, aluminum, concrete, stucco, and dri-vet.

✔ Basement: Full, partial, finished, unfinished, partially finished.

✔ Garage: Number of cars.

✔ Lot Size: 110 x 60.

✔ A brief description of property highlights: Recently updated brick Georgian 3 blocks from commuter train. First floor family room adjacent to new kitchen with granite countertops and stainless steel appliances. Master bedroom with private bath and three additional second floor bedrooms with hall bath. Two-car garage on oversized lot with professional landscaping. Freshly painted inside and out. Move in and enjoy!

✔ Contact information: Your name, phone number, property Web site address, and e-mail address.

✔ Consider including a floor plan of your home with your listing sheet.

709 Anticipate market timing to impact the sale of your home.

✔ Seller's market typically features low inventory of properties for sale, short market times, and high percentages of sale price versus list prices. Strong appreciation annually and a great market for for-sale-by-owner.

✔ Buyer's markets feature high inventories, long market times, and flat appreciation. Consider listing your home in a strong buyer's market.

710 Be realistic about the condition of your property.

✔ Property condition affects price and speed of the sale.

✔ Optimizing physical appearance and preparing in advance for marketing maximizes perceived value by agents and buyers.

✔ See Chapter 5 for preparing your home for sale.

711 Anticipate saving the selling side of a real estate agent's commission.

✔ Be prepared to pay a buyer's agent who brings a ready, willing, and able buyer to your property.

✔ Instruct all buyers' agents that you will work with them but you will remain an unrepresented seller and will pay no commission on the seller's side of the transaction.

✔ When buyers contact you directly remind them that they should bring their agent to the first showing of your property.

712 Find out if you can eliminate paying a buyers' agent commission.

✔ Determine whether a buyer who visits your open house or calls on your ad is working with an agent, if not then you will be working with an unrepresented buyer and will not have to pay any commission on the buyer's side.

✔ In some states if a buyer has a signed buyer's representation or buyer's broker agreement with an agent, they will have to compensate their agent even if they purchase a property being sold by owner.

713 Understand what a buyer's broker means.

✔ A real estate licensee represents and often has a fiduciary responsibility to the buyer.

714 Remember what a fiduciary responsibility encompasses.

✔ A business relationship that requires diligence, confidence, responsibility, and trust to the principal (client).

715 Disclose in your property advertising if you will work with real estate agents.

✔ To save yourself time, indicate in your advertising "No agents please" or "Will cooperate with agents."

716 Be realistic about the time demands of selling by owner, which will include the following:

✔ Creating a marketing plan for property.

✔ Implementing the marketing plan with the Internet, newspaper advertising, or yard signs.

✔ Setting up, confirming, and performing showing appointments for property.

✔ Hosting public open houses.

✔ Attending property inspections.

✔ Meeting buyer's lender appraiser.

✔ Accommodating additional showings for buyers to measure or brings friends and family through.

✔ Accompanying contractors or repair people for satisfying inspection issues.

✔ Facilitating final walk-through of buyers.

✔ Completing required administrative paperwork and documents.

717 Anticipate tasks when considering selling by owner.

✔ Preparing home for sale.

✔ Showing home.

✔ Understanding transaction paperwork.

✔ Legal issues.

✔ Attracting potential buyers to property.

✔ Setting the right price.

718 Research required federal, state, county, and local disclosures.

✔ Lead paint.

✔ Seller's real property disclosure report. The seller must disclose in writing all known material defects for a property.

✔ Earthquake Fault Zone. Required disclosure is located within an Earthquake Fault Zone. See county offices.

✔ Seismic Hazard Zone. Required disclosure if a property is located within a Seismic Hazard Zone. See county offices.

✔ Flood Hazard Area. Federally required disclosure for federally regulated lenders that they disclose to the purchaser in writing that a property is located in a Flood Hazard Area.

719 Hire a real estate attorney in your community to advise you on required disclosures in your state, county, and community.

720 Establish procedures for responding to inquiries about your home.

✔ Introduce yourself.

✔ Describe your home in a positive tone.

✔ Don't lie but do state the facts.

✔ State the price.

✔ Speak clearly.

✔ Mention unique features.

✔ Mention new kitchens, bathrooms, or major updating.

✔ Suggest a showing.

✔ Be available to show your home on the buyer's timeline.

✔ Don't oversell your home.

✔ Advise buyers of next public open house and property Web site address.

721 Locate local school information. Include address and school district information.

✔ Public elementary, middle, and high schools.

✔ Private elementary, middle, and high schools.

✔ Religion affiliated schools.

✔ Community and technical colleges.

✔ Special needs schools.

722 Require buyers and real estate agents to sign a guest book before viewing your home.

✔ Name, address, work, and home phone numbers.

723 Be aware of security issues when allowing strangers into your home.

✔ Carry cell phone with you and, preprogram police numbers.

✔ Ask a friend or relative to accompany you when buyers are viewing your home.

✔ Preplan escape routes before showing your home.

✔ Prequalify buyers through telephone interviews before a showing.

✔ Place valuables in safe, out-of-sight locations.

724 Determine motivation of potential buyers of your home.

✔ Ask buyers if they have a timeline to purchase and close on a new home. Buyers looking to close in six to twelve months are not motivated.

✔ Buyers looking around to see what is available are not very motivated.

✔ Relocation buyers are highly motivated.

✔ First-time buyers typically take longer to make home-buying decisions because it is their first time through the purchase process.

✔ Inquire whether buyers have a lease where they currently live, and when it expires.

✔ Nosy neighbors love public open houses.

✔ Soon-to-be-selling neighbors want to see whether your home is comparable to theirs or to see why your home is priced the way it is.

725 Learn how to qualify your buyer's ability financially to purchase your home.

✔ Have they met with a mortgage lender?

✔ Are they prequalified for a mortgage?

✔ Are they pre-approved for a mortgage?

✔ Do they have a commitment for a mortgage?

✔ Can they bring a pre-approval or qualification letter from their lender when they tour your home?

✔ Read Chapter 4 on mortgages and mortgage processes.

✔ If they are paying cash can they verify that they have the funds available to close the purchase of your home?

726 Recognize that a request for second showing of your home by the same buyers shows serious interest.

✔ Don't hover.

✔ Let buyers explore home at their own pace.

✔ Don't accompany buyers throughout entire home.

✔ Tell buyers to inspect closets, cabinets, and vanities.

✔ Don't talk through the entire showing.

✔ Let buyers ask questions.

✔ Let buyers voice possible issues.

✔ Let buyers be objective about your home.

✔ Accept compliments.

✔ Have photos of yard in summer bloom in winter.

✔ Compile list of improvements you have made to property.

727 Require all offers on your home to be in writing.

728 Develop an information sheet once you have an offer on your home.

✔ Names, home address, and phone number.

✔ Work phone and fax numbers.

✔ Cell numbers.

✔ E-mail addresses.

✔ Attorney name, phone, and fax numbers.

✔ Mortgage loan officer name, phone, and fax numbers.

729 Consider the terms of an offer.

✔ Price.

✔ Earnest money.

✔ Closing date.

✔ Possession.

✔ Mortgage contingency.

✔ Attorney approval.

✔ Inspection contingency.

✔ Tax prorations.

✔ Home sale and/or closing contingency.

✔ Personal property included or excluded.

730 Develop a negotiating checklist for every offer.

✔ Date, time offer received.

✔ Response due by.

✔ Response in writing or verbal.

✔ Price.

✔ Earnest money: amount of initial, balance amount, date balance due.

✔ Closing date.

✔ Possession date.

✔ Mortgage contingency: number of days, amount of mortgage, type (fixed, adjustable, interest only, other).

✔ Attorney approval: number of days.

✔ Inspection contingency: number of days.

✔ Tax prorations: percent seller to pay of unpaid tax bills and special assessments.

✔ Home sale and/or closing contingency: home to market and sell, is home currently listed, with who, phone number, or home under contract and waiting to close

✔ Personal property included or excluded.

✔ Your counteroffer: price, mortgage contingency, earnest money changes, inspection, attorney approval changes, closing date, possession date, personal property changes, response deadline. Date and time counteroffer delivered.

731 Study what personal property is customary in your market to be included or excluded.

✔ Refrigerator, stove, microwave, dishwasher, disposal, trash compactor.

✔ Washer, dryer.

✔ Satellite dish and system.

✔ Tacked down carpeting.

✔ All window treatments and hardware.

✔ Built-in or attached shelving.

✔ Ceiling fans(s).

✔ TV antenna system.

✔ Window air-conditioner(s).

✔ All planted vegetation.

✔ Fireplace screen(s), door(s), grate(s).

✔ Fireplace gas logs.

✔ Existing storms and screens.

✔ Security systems.

✔ Intercom systems.

✔ Central vacuum and equipment.

✔ Automatic garage door openers and transmitters.

✔ Invisible fence system, collar(s), and box.

✔ Central air-conditioning.

✔ Electronic air filtration systems.

✔ Humidifier(s).

✔ Sump pump(s).

✔ Water softener.

✔ Outdoor shed(s).

✔ Attached gas grill(s).

✔ Light fixture(s).

✔ Well and septic pumps.

732 Learn what is commonly excluded from a sale of a home in your market.

✔ Area rugs.

✔ Chandeliers.

✔ Draperies that match bedroom linens.

✔ Mirrors hung as pictures.

✔ Patio furniture.

✔ Outdoor play equipment.

✔ Family heirlooms that are attached to home.

733 Do not give legal advice to buyers of your home.

✔ You can be charged with illegal practice of law.

✔ Suggest your buyers hire an attorney to draft their offer.

734 Remember price is one of many terms of a successful offer.

✔ Investigate what percentage of list price homes have sold for in your market in the last six months.

✔ A full price offer from a buyer who can't provide a mortgage commitment is a weak buyer.

✔ Be flexible in trading price for terms, or terms for price.

✔ Some buyers will pay more for a closing date that meets their needs.

✔ Always respond to low-ball offers with a counteroffer, buyers might be testing you out on their first price offer.

735 Understand that your buyer's earnest money amount illustrates their motivation to perform the real estate contract.

✔ It is customary to have a $1,000 earnest money check with an offer.

✔ Have buyers make earnest money checks out to your attorney, with property address and earnest money in note section.

✔ It is common in some markets require a second earnest money payment within a certain period after signed acceptance of the parties. Depending on the price of the property it can be from 1% -10% of the contract price.

✔ Low earnest money pledges from buyers increases the ease of them walking away from a contract if they change their mind about moving forward.

✔ Promissory notes are common in various markets. Discuss this option with your attorney.

736 Learn what a promissory note is.

✔ A written promise to repay a debt.

737 Consider having your attorney hold all earnest monies received for the sale of your property.

738 Recognize that the closing date can kill an otherwise good offer.

739 Be aware of what is customary for possession in your market.

740 Study your buyer's mortgage contingency and its terms.

741 Be realistic about attorney approval contingencies.

742 Educate yourself about tax and other prorations in real estate contracts.

743 Familiarize yourself with home sale/closing provisions.

744 Decide which personal property you want included or excluded from the sale of your home.

Chapter 7

Selling Your Home with a Real Estate Agent

745 Contact at least three agents from different companies to view your home and prepare a Comparative Market Analysis (CMA).

746 Ask the agents you interview for their suggestions on what you could do to make your home more attractive to potential buyers.

747 Learn that a Comparative Market Analysis includes the following:

✔ A written analysis evaluating and establishing value based on homes presently on the market (active), closed homes (closed), and homes that have sold but have not closed (pending or under contract).

748 Make sure that all CMAs include at least three comparable properties in each of the three categories (active, closed, pending).

749 Check to see whether all comparable sales are from the last six months.

750 Study your real estate agent's marketing plans for your property. Look for the following elements:

✔ Internet postings on agent, brokerage, and Realtor.com Web sites.

✔ Print advertising in newspapers, magazines, and home guides.

✔ Direct mail to neighborhoods and housing centers.

✔ Multiple Listing Service.

✔ Broker-to-broker advertising.

✔ Public open houses.

✔ Broker open houses.

✔ Brokerage office tour of new listings.

751 Know that an agent should bring to a listing appointment all of the following:

✔ Comparative Market Analysis.

✔ Sample listing agreement.

✔ Agency and property disclosure documents.

✔ Sample contract documents.

✔ Sales process checklist.

✔ Marketing samples.

✔ Showing tips.

✔ Sample home checklist of features.

✔ Client testimonials from closed clients.

✔ Camera.

✔ Measuring tape.

752 Invite agents that are full time and experienced in your market based on the following criteria:

✔ Works a minimum of 50 hours per week in real estate.

✔ Has worked the last three years in your community and market.

✔ Has completed at least 20 closed transactions in each of the last three years.

753 Consider the variety of real estate brokerages, which include large national firms that bring solid name recognition to your property.

754 Be aware that smaller independent brokerages might not have the financial strength or marketing systems to promote your property.

755 Look for thorough local, regional, and national advertising placed by firms under consideration.

756   Seek out real estate professionals with the following skill set:

Real estate sales or brokers license for state in which real estate sales are practiced.

✔ Continuing education requirements met for maintaining licensure.

✔ If member of National Association of REALTORS®, mandatory ethics education completed.

✔ Knowledge of federal, state, county, and local Fair Housing laws.

✔ Professional development classes for professional designations such as GRI (Graduate REALTOR® Institute).

✔ Negotiation strategies.

✔ Home and building construction familiarity.

✔ Technology education.

✔ Sales and small business day-to-day and management education.

757   Determine whether agents who promote the fact that they have an assistant will be deferring most of your listing management to that assistant.

758   Remember you are hiring the *agent* to represent your property, not their assistant.

759   Recognize that agent assistants can be licensed or nonlicensed, which affects the amount of information that they are allowed to give out.

760   Know that assistant duties and experience focus more on administration than sales and negotiation.

761   Be realistic when making your choice for an agent to list your property.

762   Watch out for unprofessional behavior such as bad-mouthing the competition.

763 Beware of agents who try to "buy" the listing with a higher listing price than other agents.

764 Do not automatically believe an agent's offers of immediate buyers for your property only if you list with that agent.

765 When interviewing agents, ask whether they plan to be in town the crucial first three weeks your home is newly on the market.

766 Verify that the actual listing agent will host the first brokers' and public open houses.

767 Make sure that the listing agent will be available to answer agents' and consumers' questions about your property in a timely manner.

768 Request that the listing agent personally accompany showings on your new listing to provide additional familiarity of your property.

769 Understand that your signature on a listing agreement creates an agency relationship, which is a business relationship where one person (the principal or client) delegates to another person (the broker) the right to act on the principal's behalf.

770 Learn the differences in types of listing agreements as explained here:

✔ *Exclusive right to sell*: an agreement where the seller must pay the broker a commission no matter who sells the property during a specified period of time.

✔ *Exclusive agency*: a listing contract where the seller gives one agent the right to sell the property for a specified time, but reserving the right for the seller to sell the property him/her self without owing a commission.

✔ *Net listing*: where the commission is the difference between the selling price and a minimum price set by the seller.

✔ *Multiple Listing Service (MLS) only*: a broker whose only obligation to the seller is to list the property for a period in the MLS.

✔ *Open listing*: a listing that gives a broker the nonexclusive right to find a buyer. No buyer, no commission.

771
Ask to see a copy of the listing agreement before you sign, and review it with your attorney.

772
Be familiar with what will be included in a listing agreement.
✔ Property address.
✔ Commission amount.
✔ Price.
✔ Period of listing agreement.
✔ Termination conditions.
✔ Compliance with Fair Housing laws.
✔ Disclosure of property assessments.
✔ Disclosure of special assessments.
✔ Property taxes and exemptions.
✔ Property identification numbers.
✔ Dispute resolutions.

773
Remember that you can request to change the terms of your listing agreement before you sign it.

774
Feel free to negotiate the commission rate.

775
Strike documentation fees in addition to the commission charged by the brokerage. These fees are in the $100 to $400 range. Have the listing agent pay this fee.

776
Agree to a listing period for a minimum of 60 days and no longer than 120 days.

777 Give your agent some time to market and sell the property.

778 Offer to renew the agreement, but leave yourself an out to find a new agent if your property hasn't sold after four months.

779 Limit or eliminate the time that the broker will receive a commission after listing period has terminated.

780 Only pay a commission if the agent sells and closes the property during the listing period.

781 Understand that brokers cannot fix commission rates in a market. Such an act is a violation of antitrust laws.

782 Look for a lower commission structure in a seller's market with quick selling times and low costs to the broker.

783 Realize that a commission can be a fixed, stepped, or variable amount depending on market time or selling price.

784 Recognize that full service brokers' commissions nationally average about 5% to 5.5% of the selling price.

785 Learn how antitrust laws are applied to real estate commissions.

✔ Assignment of marketing territories.

✔ Property price fixing.

✔ Commission fixing.

786 Be aware that you can't strike compliance with Fair Housing laws from a listing agreement.

787

Consider listing your home as "not to be shown until _____" to gain exposure while you finish "tweaking" home remodeling or return from vacation.

✔ You have signed a listing agreement but your home is not entered in the Multiple Listing Service until a specified date.

✔ Creates exposure in the market before you are ready to implement a marketing program.

✔ Usually no sign in front of property.

788

Understand that with limited exposure, some ready, willing, and able buyers will not know of its availability.

789

Have your agent deliver "coming soon" listing information to all brokerages in your community.

790

Do not leave a property out of the MLS for more than two weeks. Check Local Board of REALTORS® rules on exempt (not in MLS) listings.

791

Consider carefully the pricing of your home.

✔ Sellers and agents can research what comparables sold for, but in the end, buyers set values in housing markets.

✔ Realistic pricing lets the market know that you are confident of the actual value of your home.

792

Recognize that trying an inflated price strategy tells the market that you're not serious.

793

Decide how much over your actual sale price you want your list price to be.

794

Understand that some buyers feel they have to negotiate as part of the purchase process.

795 Check with your agent to see what is common in your market.

796 Know that homes that are priced right and have typical styles and features sell near full price.

797 Understand that pricing in the 1% to 5% range over actual sale price is common.

798 Recognize the signs of an overpriced property:

✔ Twenty-five showings with no offers.

✔ Buyer and agent feedback from showings stating property is overpriced.

✔ Long market times.

✔ Second, third, and fourth public open houses with low attendance.

✔ Agents stigmatizing home as overpriced.

799 Accept the fact that you may need to reposition an overpriced property.

800 Have a frank and honest talk with your listing agent to determine if the overpricing was the agent's idea or one you insisted upon.

801 To reposition, set a new list price at actual market value.

802 Take the property off the market for a month to let the listing "cool off."

803 Consider bringing in a new agent to gain a fresh perspective on property marketing.

804 Decide whether underpricing a property will bring a sale in the following situations:

✔ You need a fast sale.

✔ You are placing your home in the market cycle when low numbers of buyers are looking for a home to purchase.

✔ To attract multiple offers from buyers who perceive property is undervalued and through negotiations raise sale price over list price.

805 Look for methods to send signals to the market that you are motivated seller without lowering list price such as:

✔ Offer additional commission to buyer's broker.

✔ Consider paying part or all of buyer's closing costs.

✔ Give allowances for dated decorating, bathrooms, or kitchens, old furnaces, or deteriorating concrete or roofs.

✔ Set a time deadlines to create urgency.

806 Consider friends or family members who have shown serious interest in purchasing your home as exclusions in your listing agreement.

✔ Listing exclusions name specific parties who if they enter into a contract to purchase your home, you will not have to pay your broker a commission.

✔ Listing exclusions usually have a specified time period.

✔ Some brokers don't like exclusions, but most will respect this addition to a listing agreement.

807 Be prepared to furnish to your agent the following when you sign a listing agreement.

✔ Copy of your most recent tax bill.

✔ Copy of property survey.

✔ Copies of gas, electric, and water bills from last 12 months.

✔ If condo or co-op, a copy of declarations, bylaws, minutes from association meetings; annual, quarterly or monthly assessment; and current or proposed special assessments amounts.

✔ Copy of termite warranty, if applicable.

✔ Asbestos removal certification.

✔ Copy of certification of decommissioned oil tank.

✔ Certificate of occupancy or smoke detector certificate if required by local laws.

✔ Copies of all building permits issued while you owned property.

808 Establish with any real estate agent that you will receive copies of all agreements, contracts, and documents when you sign them.

809 Recognize that your agent might suggest a premarket inspection of your home at your expense to provide the following benefits.

✔ Disclosure to you of possible buyer inspection issues.

✔ Ability to correct issues before going on market.

810 Plan ahead with cost estimates to eradicate known lead, radon, pest, asbestos, mold, or buried oil tank.

✔ Actual cost is usually lower than buyer perception of costs.

✔ Seller looks proactive on sensitive buyer issues.

811 Be prepared to refuse to allow your agent's request to be a dual agent.

✔ Not in the seller's best interest.

✔ Conflict of ethical standards for the agent.

✔ Benefits the agent at the expense of the seller and buyer.

812 Understand that a dual agent is an agent who represents both the buyer and the seller in the sale of one property.

813 Review the limitations placed on a real estate agent acting as a dual agent.

✔ Cannot disclose confidential information that the licensee may know about the clients without the client's permission.

✔ Cannot disclose the price the seller will take other than the listing price without permission of the seller.

✔ Cannot disclose the price the buyer is willing to pay without permission of the buyer.

✔ Cannot disclose a recommended or suggested price the buyer should offer.

✔ Cannot disclose a recommended or suggested price the seller should counter or accept.

814 Consider what an agent can typically do for the buyer and a seller as a dual agent.

✔ Treat all parties honestly.

✔ Provide information about the property to the buyer.

✔ Disclose all latent material defects in the property that are known to licensee.

✔ Explain real estate terms.

✔ Assist the buyer to arrange for property inspections.

✔ Explain closing costs and procedures.

✔ Assist the buyer in comparison of financing alternatives.

✔ Provide information about comparable properties that have sold so both parties may make educated decisions on what price to accept or offer.

815 Be aware of the protected classes under federal Fair Housing laws.

✔ Sex

✔ Race

✔ Religion

✔ National origin

✔ Color

✔ Mental or physical handicap

✔ Families with children under 18 years of age (familial status)

816 Keep in mind that states, counties, and cities may add additional protected classes such as:

✔ Age

✔ Occupation

✔ Sexual orientation

✔ Marital status

817 Learn the definition of *steering*, which is prohibited by federal Fair Housing laws.

✔ Steering is the directing of potential home buyers or renters to particular neighborhoods or areas based on sex, race, religion, national origin, color, mental or physical handicap, or familial status.

818 Look for the Equal Housing Opportunity poster in any real estate broker's office and marketing pieces.

✔ Failure to display the Equal Housing Opportunity poster could be considered as evidence of discrimination if a complaint is filed against the real estate broker.

819 Remember that Fair Housing laws apply to most residential housing of one to four units with only a few exceptions.

820 Request that your agent prepare a virtual tour of your property.

✔ A 360-degree digitized video tour of your home.

✔ Virtual tour placed on agent and brokerage Web site.

✔ Buyers can preview your home 24/7.

✔ Showcases your home dramatically and creates buyer excitement.

✔ Cost to agent: $75 to $300.

821 Know the competition in your market when your home is for sale.

822 Attend public open houses for properties similar to yours.

823 View virtual tours of the competition on the Internet.

824 Track print advertising type and frequency of the competition versus that provided on your property.

825 Establish what your competition is based on the following:

✔ Priced similarly.

✔ Total room count within one room plus or minus.

✔ Bathrooms should match or be very close.

✔ Age should be within five years.

✔ Condition should be similar.

✔ Location the same.

✔ Style and features close.

✔ Updating and remodeling similar.

✔ Garage or off-street-parking equivalent.

826 Understand why your real estate agent might not want you to be present when showing your home.

✔ Allows buyers the freedom to comment on your home.

✔ Buyers are more willing to take their time and investigate features or systems.

✔ Buyers are more likely to discuss how they would place their furniture or decorate.

827 Remember to be ready for showings of your home by following this checklist:

✔ During daylight open all draperies, shades, and blinds. Natural light is at the top of most buyers' wish lists.

✔ At night turn on all the lights. Dark homes are not inviting.

✔ Have photos of the garden or before and after photos of major remodeling you have undertaken.

✔ Use feature cards around your home to reinforce home benefits such as air-conditioning or nearby parks or playgrounds in the winter.

✔ Clean sinks, bathrooms before each showing.

✔ Vacuum rugs and carpets before each showing.

✔ Wash dirty dishes and put away.

✔ Empty waste baskets and trash

✔ Put away clothes and personal items.

✔ Organize mail, magazines, and newspapers.

✔ Fold towels and make beds.

✔ Eliminate offensive odors.

✔ Refrain from smoking in your home while it is on market and available for showing.

✔ Keep landscaping neat and mowed. Sweep driveways and sidewalks.

✔ Shovel snow.

✔ Pick up litter on property.

✔ Pick up animal droppings in yard and keep litter boxes clean and fresh.

✔ Minimize religious effects.

✔ Put sexually explicit materials away.

✔ Clean sells!

828 Recognize that, as a seller, it is common to feel uncomfortable about having strangers in your home.

829 Ask your listing agent to accompany all showings of your home to monitor buyers and their agents.

830 Know that you can ask to not have a lockbox placed on your home.

831 Remove and store off-site personal belonging and furniture that you don't want strangers to view.

832 Make plans for removing or controlling your pets during showings.

✔ Some buyers have pet allergies.

✔ Barking can be threatening and distracting to buyers.

✔ You might feel comfortable with your pet, but some buyers dislike loose animals at showings.

✔ Annoying pets can shorten showing times and work against property marketing.

833 Welcome a buyer's agent who asks to do a "preview" showing prior to making an appointment to bring the potential buyer.

✔ The agent has to see whether your home meets the clients' home search criteria, before bringing the clients to view it.

834 Remember that the first two weeks your home is on market will focus the most buyer attention on your property.

✔ New inventory attracts agents and buyers.

✔ Your listing might motivate buyers to start a home search.

✔ Fresh inventory can reinvigorate a sluggish market.

835 Pay attention to the different aspects of showing feedback your agent will receive from buyers' agents who have shown your property.

✔ Listing agent will follow up with buyers' agent to see what the agents and their clients thought of your home.

✔ Can be positive or negative.

836 Anticipate the different types of showing feedback.

✔ *First day out* = just started home search, could come back.

✔ *They're thinking about taking another look* = second showings usually show elevated interest, but if it isn't how they remembered it, it's over.

✔ *Loved it* = looks like they could be writing an offer.

✔ *It's on their short list of homes to buy* = find out what your competition is.

✔ *They have some questions* = good sign, serious interest.

✔ *They want to bring their parents back* = family members can build confidence in or kill a home sale.

✔ *Nice first floor* (in a two story home) = the second floor layout or number of bedrooms on second floor didn't work.

✔ *Too many projects* = buyers are not prepared to do major updating or remodeling.

✔ *Too much wallpaper* = if you hear this comment a lot, consider having it removed.

✔ *Poor room flow* = hard to change.

✔ *Tired or needs tender loving care* = buyers can't see past dirt, clutter, or damaged walls, floors, or fixtures.

✔ *Overpriced* = if you hear this comment a lot, consider lowering your price.

✔ *Just didn't work* = the buyers might not have clear home parameters.

✔ *Nice house, wrong location* = the house worked but buyers have different location needs than your home offers.

837 Recognize that second showings can't be managed.

✔ The buyers' agent can best overcome buyer objections because of his or her experience with the buyers, rather than your agent or the sellers.

✔ Some buyers like to come back at night if their first showing was during daylight and vice versa.

838 Let the buyers' agent show and lead the showing, because of that agent's knowledge of the features and benefits the clients are interested in.

839 Give the buyers the freedom to voice issues and address them.

✔ You may have had the same concerns and have found a solution.

840 Let the buyers make themselves comfortable. Have your agent offer them a chair or to take off their jackets.

841 Allow the buyers to take photos of your home to share with friends, family, or coworkers.

842 If the buyers have questions that your agent can't answer, don't lie, find out the questions and get back to their agent with answers.

843 Plan ahead for your first public open house.

✔ Typically last 2–4 hours.
✔ Sellers should not attend.

844 Ask to see sign-in sheet from the open house.

845 Insist that your listing agent host all open houses because they are most familiar with your home's features and benefits.

846 Offer open house guests cookies and coffee or bottled water. (The smell of baking is always a plus!)

847 Expect the neighbors to check out your home. Don't be offended—they may know someone interested in moving to your neighborhood.

848 Review the open house premarketing planned by your agent; a good plan will help to significantly increase attendance.

849 Make your home "sparkle" for the open house: clean, neat, no clutter, fresh flowers.

850 Require your real estate agent to host a brokers' open house.

✔ Allows an agent in your market to preview new listings for their buyers.

✔ Builds buzz for your home in agent community.

✔ Offer lunch or gift certificates to build agent traffic.

✔ You can attend brokers' open house; it's good to hear agent feedback.

851 Recognize that buyers will ask about the market time of your property.

✔ The number of days your property has been in the listing service and available to all brokers in the market.

✔ Some buyers will think a long time on the market indicates you are willing to cut your price.

852 Find out average market time for properties similar to yours as a benchmark to gauge additional marketing, open houses, or price reductions.

853 Be sure that all offers on your home are in writing.

✔ Verbal offers are not enforceable in most states.

✔ Research your state license laws.

854 Anticipate that your first offers will be often the strongest.

✔ New inventory and low market times create urgency in buyers to write strong offers.

✔ Sometimes it's hard to believe, but agents know that often the first offer will be the best one and you will wish later that you had accepted it!

855 Establish what is customary in your market: will you be receiving an "offer to purchase" or a "real estate contract" on your property?

✔ *Offer*: a proposal to originate a contract.

✔ *Contract*: parties agree to do or not do defined legal acts and consideration is exchanged.

856 Study negotiation tips before receiving an offer on your home.

✔ Negotiations are about understanding the other side's psychology, motivations, and needs.

✔ Good communication early in negotiations could bypass posturing that creates ill will.

✔ Unresolved minor issues can fester and become barriers to major issues.

857 Do not propose terms if you can't live with them; be aware of what you say and when you say it.

858 After reaching an agreement with the other side, talk about implementation of the transaction process.

✔ If you need time to think about an offer, ask for the buyers to let you respond by a certain date and time to their offer.

✔ Less is more in successful negotiations. Wearing people out makes them less agreeable.

859 Study the options available for you in responding to an offer.

✔ *Refuse the offer with invitation for buyers to submit a new offer*: the offer was low but you want to leave the door open for buyers to come back with a stronger offer. Best used when the spread between the offer price and the list price is more than 10%.

✔ *Refuse the offer*: when a low-ball offer (more than 15% less than list price) is presented.

✔ *Refuse to respond to the offer*: a low-ball offer of more than 20% less than list price.

✔ *Counteroffer*: the response to an offer by the seller or the buyer after the original offer.

✔ *Accept the offer*: the seller and buyer have accepted all terms of an offer or contract. (Also called acceptance.)

860 Look for your agent to set some ground rules when you receive multiple offers.

✔ Your agent should present all offers to you promptly.

✔ Present all offers to you in the order they were submitted.

✔ Make the buyers and their agents aware of your procedures for handling multiple offers.

✔ Provide all parties with the same information.

✔ Keep all parties informed at all stages of the process.

✔ Inquire of losers in a multiple offer if they want their offer used as a backup offer.

861 Learn how a backup offer can help you.

✔ Having a backup can force your first accepted offer to release contingencies and proceed to closing.

✔ Provides a "Plan B" if the first offers falls apart during attorney and or inspection review.

862 Consider your options if you receive multiple offers at one time for your home.

✔ Compare the strengths and weaknesses of all offers on a worksheet provided by your real estate agent.

✔ You can negotiate each offer separately or respond to all with a request for their "highest and best offer."

863 Understand what a "take it or leave it" offer implies.

✔ You can accept the offer.

✔ You can reject the offer.

✔ You *can* counteroffer the "take it or leave it" offer.

864 Have an attorney review all contracts on the sale of your home *before* you sign.

865 Take special notice of the earnest money being offered with the contract.

✔ A strong price and weak earnest money, down payment, or credit could indicate a lower probability of buyer's ability to close the transaction.

✔ Earnest money shows the buyer's willingness to perform a contract and go to closing.

✔ It is common in some markets for the earnest money to be delivered in two steps. First an amount is delivered with the contract or offer and a second amount is delivered after inspection and attorney periods have expired or issues resolved to both parties' satisfaction.

866 Request mortgage pre-approval or commitment and contact information to verify buyer's ability to receive financing.

867 Do they have a home to sell? Is it already on market? Buyers needing equity from their current home to purchase yours is typical. Look for their property to be listed, priced correctly, and typical in style, condition, and features for market.

868 Have they sold their home but it has not closed yet? Buyers have a contract on their home but are waiting for the closing. Research the viability of their contract closing as stated.

869 Pay special attention to any requested contingencies in the contract.

✔ The longer a contingency period, the less probability of the buyer exercising its use.

✔ Request business days for contingencies. Business days are Monday through Friday excluding holidays.

✔ Attorney and inspection contingencies should run at the same time and for no more than seven business days.

870 Be aware of the different types of buyers' home sale contingency terms.

✔ Successful sale and close of buyers' property.

✔ Successful closing of buyers' property. (Property already sold.)

✔ 24-, 36-, 48- or 72-hour kick-out clause: A contingency in a real estate contract that allows a home sale or closing clause to be dropped from the terms of a contract when executed by the seller upon receipt of another offer or contract by a buyer. The buyer after receiving notice from the seller has to remove contingency or cancel contract.

✔ Home sale or closing kick-outs should have dated timelines when contingency is in effect.

871   Be realistic about anticipating buyers' remorse in the following situations:

✔ If buyers feel they overpaid due to a multiple offer scenario.

✔ First-time home-buyers ask themselves "What did we do?"

✔ One person in a couple liked the property more than the other.

✔ Another home comes on market that better suits their home parameters.

872   Recognize that you might have seller's remorse about the following:

✔ Selling the family home.

✔ Agreeing to sell for less than you wanted.

✔ Including terms that you feel are unacceptable.

✔ Feeling rushed to move and vacate house.

873   Call your attorney immediately during attorney approval period if you have serious seller's remorse and discuss your alternatives.

874   Be aware that the buyers of your home might want to meet you.

✔ Postpone until after the successful written acceptance of a real estate contract.

✔ Request that your agent and the buyer's agent attend all meetings between sellers and buyers.

875   Understand the timing to stop showings of your home after accepting a contract.

✔ Typically showings end at the successful conclusion of the attorney and inspection period.

876   Learn your available options for issues that arise from the buyer's home inspection.

✔ Agree to repair items with a licensed technician before closing.

✔ Agree to credit the buyers for them to have items repaired after closing.

✔ Refuse to have item repaired or to issue a credit at closing.

✔ Review inspection issues and possible resolutions with your real estate agent.

877 Research what options you have when the buyers want to nullify your contract after all contingencies have been removed.

✔ Contact a real estate attorney immediately.

878 Become familiar with your options if your home does not appraise for the sale price by your buyer's lender.

✔ Buyer must make up the difference between contract sales price and appraised price.

✔ Contract sale price amended to appraisal price.

✔ Contact your attorney.

879 Be prepared for the buyer's final walk-through before closing.

✔ All personal property removed.

✔ Broom clean.

✔ Leave manuals for appliances staying with house.

✔ Leave warranties for home fixtures, appliances, or services.

✔ Leave automatic garage door openers.

✔ Prepare a list of home service providers and contact information.

880 Make every effort to avoid the following potential problems at closing.

✔ Personal property purchased by buyers but not at property for final walk-through.

✔ Damage done to property between buyer's last visit and final walk-through.

✔ Inspection issues agreed to be repaired before closing but not done.

✔ Home dirty or containing unwanted personal property of seller.

881 Recognize the potential problems at closing on the buyer's side.

✔ Buyer not having enough funds to close loan or contract.

✔ Buyer bringing personal check instead of certified check.

✔ Buyer or seller not having photo identification at closing.

✔ Missing or incorrect loan documents.

✔ Title company information or funding of buyers' mortgage arriving late at escrow.

882 Learn what a *dry closing* means.

✔ All required documents are signed between seller and buyer but proceeds not distributed to transaction participants.

883 Anticipate whether you will hold over (remain in the property) in your home or give possession at closing.

✔ If you hold over you will rent back from the buyers at a minimum daily rate equal to their daily cost for mortgage principal, interest, taxes, insurance, and if applicable, assessments.

✔ Possession at closing means you will surrender all keys and have removed all personal property when buyers take title to property.

884 All your loans recorded against your property will be paid off at closing.

✔ First mortgage.

✔ Second mortgage.

✔ Home equity loans.

885 Be realistic about the level of interest when you place your home for sale between November 15 and December 31.

✔ Low level of buyers during this period.

✔ Exception is in resort markets.

✔ Buyers will discount your property price if you listed in November and have high market times in January.

886 Wait and list your home in January after holidays are over.

887 Have realistic expectations of your real estate agent.

✔ If you insist on overpricing your home, even the best agents will have problems selling it.

✔ If you make your home difficult to show, your agent can't sell it.

✔ Real estate agents aren't housekeepers; your role in your partnership with your agent is to keep your home clean and ready to show.

✔ If your agent didn't sell you your home and it has a poor location, layout, or style, don't ask them to fix the unfixable.

✔ Most agents work seven days a week, at times they could be tired, have schedule conflicts, or be ill.

✔ Communicate your concerns in a timely manner to your agent.

888 Research what your options are when you're not satisfied with your real estate agent.

✔ Review your listing agreement for termination clause.

✔ Share your concerns about your agent with the agent's managing broker.

✔ Site specific situations where you feel your agent failed to meet your expectations.

889 Understand your seller's "bill of rights" concerning what to expect from your agent.

✔ Timely return of phone calls or e-mails.

✔ Communication showing feedback and ongoing market strategy.

✔ Professional attitude.

✔ Respect of ethics, Fair Housing, and license laws.

✔ Adequate marketing of property through Internet, newspapers, direct mail, and open houses.

✔ No personality conflict.

PART 3
Moving

Jumping Joe's
Moving Service

Chapter 8
Corporate Relocation:
Understanding the Process

890 **Take the time educate yourself about the corporate relocation process.**

✔ Read the relocation policy and benefits you have received from your employer in its entirety before you sell or purchase a home.

✔ Research property values in your new community before you negotiate compensation from your employer in your new position.

891 **Learn what is included in your relocation policy.**

✔ Destination services: refers transferee to real estate agents in their destination community to make informed new home, community, and school decisions.

✔ Home sale: refers transferee in their departure home to real estate agents to coordinate home value and property marketing and sale assistance.

✔ Transportation services: refers transferee to preferred vendors for the prompt and safe delivery of household goods from departure home to new home location.

✔ Temporary housing assistance: allows for financial assistance to transferee in new location to rent housing until permanent housing is found.

✔ Familiarization and home-buying travel: allows for reimbursement of travel costs for you and your family to educate yourselves about community and home purchase options in your destination community.

892 **Research what your departure and destination real estate agent can and can't do under your policy.**

893 **Remember that real estate agents are strongly discouraged by relocation companies to contact the employee or transferee's employer on their behalf.**

894   Accept that real estate agents are strongly discouraged from having access to or reading a transferee's personal relocation policy.

895   Consider your relocation policy benefits are usually negotiable. Your employer wants you to be satisfied through the relocation process.

896   Smooth relocations ease transferee's stress and provide productive returns to employer.

897   Be aware that your relocation policy will be executed by a third-party company.

898   Learn what a third-party company does.

✔ A relocation company is hired by the employee's employer to coordinate an employee's move to new location designated by the employer.

899   Remember the third-party company's principal client is your employer.

✔ Your employer compensates the third-party company for the sale of your departure home, destination home, travel and moving expenses.

900   Understand that you are the third-party company's customer.

✔ Your relocation manager will communicate your relocation needs, problems, or questions to their client, your employer.

901   Recognize that your relocation manager at the third-party company will drive your relocation experience.

902   Remember if you are not satisfied with your relocation manager, ask to be assigned a new manager through your human resources department.

903 Recognize that your relocation manager is your advocate through the entire relocation process.

904 Anticipate that your relocation manager, destination specialist, or property specialist might not be familiar with your departure or new community.

✔ Most national relocation third-party companies are in select cities and states.

✔ With the large number of communities and real estate markets nationally, relocation managers and property specialists won't be always be up-to-date and familiar with recent market trends in your departure or destination markets.

905 Understand that your property specialist reports to his or her relocation manager.

✔ The property specialist is only responsible for the transferee's sale of their home in the departure city.

906 Be aware that your destination specialist reports to his or her relocation manager.

✔ The destination specialist is only responsible for the transferee's purchase, lease, or temporary housing in the destination community.

907 Be realistic in your expectations of your relocation manager, destination specialist, or property specialist.

✔ Each specialist or manager is working with many transferees at one time.

✔ Be aware of time zone differences between their office location and yours in their ability to communicate.

✔ Only your employer can change your relocation policy and its benefits.

908 Learn the difference between marketing assistance and home sale buyout in your departure home.

✔ Marketing assistance empowers the transferee to market and sell a home before pursuing a home sale buyout.

✔ A transferee can exercise a home sale buyout at an appraisal price by the third-party company. The buyout and direct home selling costs are charged back to the employer. The buyout allows the transferee to use their departure home equity to purchase a home in their destination community.

✔ Not all relocation policies offer a home sale buyout as a benefit.

✔ All home sale buyouts have a guaranteed price offer.

909 Recognize what the direct home selling costs are to your relocation company.

✔ Carrying costs, loss on sale, repairs and improvements, commission, closing costs, principal, interest, taxes and insurance, interest on equity loans, and utilities.

910 Understand what a guaranteed offer means under your relocation policy.

✔ The amount, after appraisals, the employer will offer the transferring employee for his or her property.

✔ Typically the price offer is based on the average of two or three independent appraisals completed by licensed or certified appraisers.

911 Become familiar with how your relocation policy defines marketing assistance.

✔ Develop and implement with a real estate agent a marketing plan to obtain a sale for the highest price in the shortest time.

✔ Marketing assistance is period of time in which the transferee may market his or her property, typically 45, 60 or 90 days, as directed by the third-party company's contract with the employer.

✔ The transferee typically must have three real estate agents summit their broker's price opinion (BPO) of the property, broker's market analysis (BMA), and comparative market analysis (CMA).

912 Become familiar with the broker's price opinion.

✔ The real estate broker's opinion of the expected final net sale price, determined prior to the acquisition of property.

913 Educate yourself about the Broker's Market Analysis.

✔ The real estate broker's opinion of the expected final net sale price, determined after the acquisition of property by the third party company.

✔ The broker completes the Employee Relocation Council (ERC) Brokers Market Analysis and Strategy Report, A form copyrighted by the Employee Relocation Council that is used by brokers to analyze a home that is to be in a corporate relocation policy. The form studies the transferee's property: its condition, competition, and future marketability.

914 Evaluate all three of the comparative market analysis of your home carefully.

915 Request factual analysis from active, pending, and sold comparable properties in the last six months used to provide market information to the seller and assist the real estate broker in securing a sale at the highest price in the shortest time.

916 Require from all agents you interview a property marketing plan of your property that includes Internet, print, broker-to-broker, and direct mail advertising. Office agent tour, and broker and public open houses are a must.

917 If the three suggested listing prices vary widely, refer to your third-party company appraised price (AP).

918 Understand for listing agents to represent your property they will pay referral fee of 20% to 45% of their commission. The listing broker pays the referral fee to the relocation company at closing.

919 These referrals fees are used to offset the cost to your employer of relocating you.

920 Determine that you can use your agent of choice during the marketing assistance period. You should be aware that your relocation company will require you to have at least one other real estate agent review your property and deliver an Employee Relocation Council Broker's Market Analysis and Strategy Report.

921 Recognize that your relocation company will require you to complete a multipage property disclosure statement on your home.

922 Relocation company homeowner disclosure statement protects the relocation company from liability because they have not occupied the property and have thus no knowledge of its condition.

923 The home sellers' property disclosure statement lists all known defects on their property to the relocation company and prospective buyers.

924 Learn what the appraised price determines.

✔ The price the third-party relocation company offers (under most contracts) to the seller for his or her property, generally the average of two or more independent appraisals.

925 Deciding to exercise your right to a home sale buyout.

✔ Your marketing assistance period has expired.

✔ You have received a contract on your home.

✔ You need equity in your departure home for your destination purchase.

926 Terminating your listing agreement at the end of a marketing assistance period.

✔ Determine the actual list date with current real estate broker by reviewing your listing agreement.

✔ Exercise your broker exclusion clause. The broker exclusion clause protects the seller from having to pay a broker's commission in the event that the seller (transferee) accepts a home sale buyout from his or her employer. Most exclusion clauses state that the broker will only receive a commission after the sale of the transferee's home has been closed between seller and buyer. These clauses also state that the seller reserves the right to sell the property to the relocation company or employer.

✔ Terminate your listing agreement in writing with your real estate broker.

927 Receive a contract on your home during your marketing assistance period.

✔ You will remain the primary decision maker and negotiate the contract on the sale of your home to a mutually agreeable conclusion with the buyer.

✔ You will NOT sign the contract or purchase agreement.

✔ The third-party relocation company is legally responsible to follow Internal Revenue Service (IRS) regulations in an arm's-length transaction.

928 Learn about *amended value*.

✔ Actual sale price after the seller successfully markets and sells home through the broker of his or her choice.

✔ The sale is turned over to the third-party relocation company for closing, and the guaranteed offer is amended or changed.

929 Remember that most relocation companies will not allow you to accept some terms in your negotiations on an offer to purchase for your home.

930 The majority of relocation companies will not accept an offer contingent on the sale of the any of the buyer's property.

931 Most relocation companies will not accept any provisions in an offer for escrow accounts or tax prorations after the closing of the contract for purchase.

932 Learn what *tax prorations* mean in the sale or purchase of a property. Tax prorations is the division of unpaid property taxes between the seller and a buyer of a property.

933 Be aware that the buyer of your property will be required to sign an inspection rider provided by your relocation company.

✔ Inspection rider: condition to purchase agreement between third-party relocation company and buyer of transferee's property stating that property is being sold "as is." All inspection reports conducted by the third-party companies are disclosed to the buyer, and it is the buyer's duty to do his or her own inspections and tests.

934 Appreciate why your relocation company and employer will strictly adhere to the Internal Revenue Services definition of an arm's-length transaction.

935 Remember that you cannot accept any earnest money or down payments from the buyer in a relocation situation. All earnest or down payments should be directed to the listing broker in an arm's length transaction.

936 Be aware that your relocation company coordinates the transfer of title to the buyer(s).

937 You cannot sign an offer or a purchase agreement in an arm's-length transaction. A representative of the relocation company will sign the offer or agreement.

938 The arm's length transaction establishes that any employee in a employer-provided relocation policy who desires to utilize the amended value program and who lists their property with a real estate broker shall include a suitable exclusion clause in the listing agreement whereby the listing agreement is terminated upon the sale of the home to the third-party or relocation company.

939 Plan ahead in a arm's-length transaction that you enter into a binding contract with the relocation company (contract of sale).

940 Learn the definition for a *contract of sale*:
✔ Agreement between third-party relocation company and the seller (transferee), whereby the third-party company purchases property owned by the seller.

941 Recognize in an arm's-length transaction after the contract of sale has been accepted by the relocation company and after you have vacated and given possession of your home to the relocation company, the rights of ownership pass to the relocation company.

942 Understand the implication of the *vacate date*.
✔ Date on which the seller (transferee) vacates the property, generally the date when property expense responsibility by the transferee ends and the third-party company assumes ownership for the property through a buyout.

943 Realize that you relinquish any discretion over the subsequent sale of the home by your relocation company in an arm's-length transaction.

944 Remember that your contract of sale with the relocation company at the higher price is unconditional and not contingent on the potential buyers obtaining a mortgage commitment or any event in an arm's-length transaction.

945 Be aware that the relocation company enters into a separate listing agreement, relisting the property with a real estate broker to assist with the resale of the property in an arm's length transaction.

946 Understand when you exercise your home sale buyout, the property will be relisted with another broker and be entered into the relocation company's inventory.

✔ Relist: property that was listed with another broker but relisted with current broker.

947 Learn what a *relocation inventory property is.*

✔ A transferee's property aquired by a third-party relocation company through an executed contract of sale with the transferee.

948 Remember that the relocation company enters into an agreement with a buyer to purchase the home. This agreement is separate and not related to your agreement to sell your home to the relocation company in an arm's-length transaction.

949 In an arm's-length transaction, the purchase price paid by a buyer to your relocation company is not related to or has no effect on the price you received for your home by the relocation company.

950 Become familiar with the role of your destination specialist.

✔ Conducts destination needs assessment.

✔ Assigns destination real estate agent to you.

✔ Coordinates home buying and community and school familiarization trips.

✔ Coordinates temporary housing in destination community.

951   Request an information packet on your destination community from your destination real estate agent, which should include the following information:

✔ Schools, test scores, childcare options.

✔ Maps.

✔ Community, sports, and recreation.

✔ Shopping, restaurant, concert venues, and theatre guides.

✔ Utility contact information.

✔ Crime statistics, local government, federal government, drivers license testing centers.

✔ Chamber of commerce, annual events, places of interest.

✔ Banks and financial service providers.

✔ Cable, Internet provider, high-speed access, rates, multiple carriers.

✔ Public transportation, buses, trains, subways, ferries, airlines.

✔ Health, country, and yacht clubs.

✔ Medical, dental, mental, and geriatric health.

✔ Property tax rates, reassessment cycles.

952   Anticipate what you want to accomplish on your home finding or community familiarization trips.

✔ Determine how many days you will be in the destination community.

✔ Prioritize neighborhoods and communities you want to see.

✔ Determine how many homes you would like to tour.

✔ Establish how many days you want to be on your own versus working with a real estate agent.

✔ Determine special needs assessments for private schools, foods and diet availability, handicap accessibility, etc.

953   Understand what the first day with your agent should include.

✔ Area tour of selected communities.

✔ Drive-by of schools applicable to your children.

✔ Drive-by of public transportation locations.

✔ Drive-by of shopping, medical, and recreation facilities.

✔ Viewing homes that meet your search parameters, including price.

954 Recognize that your real estate agent will be assigned to you by the relocation company.

955 Verify that your agent is relocation certified. National relocation companies certify agents who have taken training exclusive to the needs of clients moving at the request of their employer.

956 Be aware that if you do not feel comfortable with the agent assigned to you, you can ask your destination services specialist to assign you to a new agent.

957 Remember that the agent who is assigned to assist you in your home search and purchase will pay the relocation company a referral fee of 20% to 45% of their commission on any home you purchase.

958 Look for your agent to prepare a buyer's broker market analysis. This analysis should include at least three active. pending, and sold properties comparable to the one you will be drafting a contract for.

959 Inquire of your assigned agent whether they can assist you in your home search if you want to change or expand communities in your search. Most agents are focused in the communities where they are comfortable and knowledgeable in working with buyers.

960 Ask your destination services specialist to reassign you to a new agent if you have made decisions that have changed your community needs and profile.

961 Consider having two agents assigned to work with you if you are considering different communities in a regional area.

962 Determine local real estate customs when an offer to purchase is drafted.

963 Inquire about contract riders, state disclosures, closing costs, real estate attorneys, earnest money deposits, escrow, and title.

964 Research contract customs regarding attorney, inspection, and mortgage contingencies. The number of days or business days that are customary varies from market to market.

965 Understand which of the following market types you will be purchasing a home in: a buyer's, balanced, or seller's market.

966 Consider that a buyer's market has abundant home inventory and longer than average days on market.

967 Look for a balanced market to feature average days on market and sufficient home inventory to meet buyer's needs.

968 Be realistic in a seller's market that has low inventory of homes for sale, short days on market, and in some cases multiple offers (buyers) for the same property.

969 Ask your real estate agent to explain how days on market (DOM) or market time (MT) is calculated in the community you wish to purchase in.

970 Be aware that in some real estate markets, the DOM might not accurately reflect the true days on market.

✔ Inquire if the local Multiple Listing Service gives market time from the day the property was posted in the service, or rolls the clock back to zero when the property has a price or change in listing broker or other factors.

✔ Ask your agent to provide you with a property history report from the Multiple Listing Service.

971
Verify resale probability on any home you are interested in purchasing. Most corporate transferees should select a property that offers parameters that meet the typical home buyer needs for their community.

✔ Avoid architectural and floor plan styles that don't conform to local tastes.

✔ Busy streets, railroad tracks, and power lines are potential resale problems.

✔ Adjacent hospitals, fire and police stations, and shopping centers discourage some buyers.

✔ Overimproved, most expensive, and largest home in area will add considerable market days when you are selling these homes.

✔ Research common number of bedrooms, bathrooms, family rooms, garages, and so on for your market.

972
Research in your relocation policy what household goods are covered for moving to your destination home.

973
Study or ask your destination services specialist if your policy covers the shipping of recreational vehicles, number of automobiles, boats, lawn tractors, and similar large items. These items are not covered by all policies and the cost to ship them to the destination home is paid by the transferee.

974
Determine whether your relocation policy covers the cost of packing and moving of fine art, pianos, organs, and antiques.

✔ Ask about temporary climate-controlled storage of fine art, pianos, organs, and antiques if you need to store these items before you receive possession of your new home.

975
Determine how long your policy covers temporary storage of all your household goods if possession is delayed in your destination home.

976
Recognize that it is customary in relocation policies to have temporary storage of household goods for a minimum of 90 days after vacating your departure home.

977   Remember to negotiate any unusual household goods moving or storage requirements at the first stages of your current or new job transfer or promotion.

978   Anticipate that you will need temporary housing in your destination community before you locate or close on a new home. This housing could be in a all-suite hotel, furnished rental apartment, or single-family home.

979   Find out if pets are allowed with you in temporary housing.

980   Accept that if you are single and are in the process of relocating for your employer that you face the additional challenge of administrating your departure home and your destination home yourself.

✔ Time management and organizational skills will help diminish your relocation-related stress.

✔ Occasionally the overlap of job responsibilities in your departure job position and transitioning into your destination job position coupled with the coordination of the sale and a purchase of a home can be daunting even for experienced single transferees.

981   Be aware of the special needs children have before, during, and after a corporate relocation.

✔ Remember to be available and understanding of your children's needs.

✔ Acknowledge both the positive and negative feelings, and keep their daily routines as normal as possible.

✔ Once you have selected your new home, make an appointment to take your children through. Show them their new bedrooms and talk about how they would like to personalize it.

✔ Take your children to their new school and have the administrator show you around. Locate their classroom, locker, and lunchroom so they can visualize themselves in the school environment.

✔ Locate community and neighborhood parks and recreation areas. Plan an outing and involve the whole family.

✔ Plan a moving party for your children and their friends; it will provide them with an event to say good-bye.

✔ Soon after you have moved into your destination home, introduce yourself and your children to your neighbors and their children. During introductions, invite neighborhood children to your home for a play date.

✔ Give your children time to acclimate to your new home, community, and school.

✔ Some children take up to one year to feel comfortable in new surroundings.

982 Your spouse or partner needs assistance adjusting to your destination community and employment.

✔ Ask your relocation manager if trailing spouse benefits are part of your relocation policy.

✔ Negotiate trailing spouse benefits when you negotiate your relocation policy.

✔ Some employment benefits for trailing spouses include paying a job finder's fee, finding employment within the transferee's company in the destination job market, or finding employment outside the transferee's company in the destination job market.

Chapter 9
Moving On:
How to Make the Best of Your Move

983 Keep in mind that being organized and efficient during your move will help reduce your stress level.

984 Research moving days and times that are the least popular.
✔ Weekdays.
✔ September through April.
✔ First three weeks of a month.

985 Start a filing system to organize related moving expenses and documents.
✔ Three-inch thick three-ring binders.
✔ Filing tote box with handle.
✔ Portable fireproof safety box.
✔ Create a floor plan of your new house to organize furniture and box distribution on move-in day.

986 Start preparing for your physical move six weeks before your move-out date.
✔ Reserve your self-move truck.
✔ Schedule help for moving day if you are moving yourself.
✔ Call three professional moving companies for quotes.
✔ Reserve self-storage space if needed.
✔ Plan date for moving sale.
✔ Arrange for school transcripts to be forwarded to new school.
✔ Find and gather auto licensing and registration documents.

✔ Ask for copies of medical and dental records.

✔ Locate birth certificates, wills, deeds, and other legal documents.

✔ Accumulate stock certificates and other financial documents.

✔ Cancel or transfer club memberships.

✔ Cancel charge accounts at local stores.

✔ Schedule service for all automobiles in household.

✔ Order preprinted address labels for your new address.

987 Plan ahead for your move five weeks before moving day.

✔ Begin pricing and cleaning items for garage sale.

✔ Register children in new school.

✔ Verify with insurance agent that your possessions will be covered during your move.

✔ Obtain new homeowners and automobile insurance in your destination community.

988 Be realistic; start packing four weeks before moving day.

✔ Start packing off-season and holiday items.

✔ Place your ad for your garage or moving sale.

✔ Mail your change of address cards.

✔ Contact gas, oil, electric, water, telephone, cable TV, newspaper, and trash collection companies for service disconnect/connect at your old and new addresses.

✔ Arrange for final readings on gas, electric, and water meters.

✔ Start using canned and frozen foods that you do not want to move.

989 Make sure you have adequate packing supplies.

✔ Boxes.

✔ Tape/tape gun.

✔ Bubble wrap.

✔ Packing peanuts.

✔ Packing paper, no newsprint.

✔ Box labels.

✔ Box inventory forms.

✔ Do not move/pack or fragile labels.

✔ Labels for items you will need immediately or during move.

✔ Black markers.

✔ Blankets.

990   Become familiar with the proper way to pack boxes.

✔ Use only clean boxes.

✔ Verify boxes from stores or work don't have insects in them.

✔ Use brightly colored tissue paper to pack small items that could be thrown out with other types of packing materials.

✔ Use small boxes for heavy items such as books.

✔ Pack hardware related to item in reclosable bag with related item.

991   Be aware of hazardous materials that can't be moved by professional movers.

✔ Cleaning fluids.

✔ Gasoline.

✔ Nail polish and remover.

✔ Paint, varnish, stains, and thinners.

✔ Kerosene.

✔ Oil.

✔ Bottle gas.

✔ Aerosol cans.

✔ Ammunition.

✔ Explosives.

✔ Corrosives.

992   Designate a color for each room of your home.

✔ Place box number on each color-coded label.

✔ Keeping like items together will make finding an item easier.

✔ Have a hardware box for special cables, cords, and furniture parts.

993   Anticipate what you need to do three weeks before moving.

✔ Hold garage or moving sale.

✔ After moving sale call charity organization to pick up leftover items from sale.

✔ Continue packing items that you will not need before or during move.

✔ Open new bank accounts in destination community.

✔ Take pets to veterinarian for check-up and copies of their records.

✔ Arrange for baby-sitter for moving day.

✔ Arrange services for special needs such as disabled or elderly.

✔ Make backups of all computer files.

994 Recognize what you will need to accomplish two weeks before moving day.

✔ Contact friends or family who have borrowed items from you and ask for their return before your moving date.

✔ Continue packing items that you will not need before or during move.

✔ Schedule special trash pickup after moving day.

✔ Clean out wood-burning fireplaces.

✔ Clean barbeque grills.

✔ Return library books, rental tapes.

✔ Pick up any photo processing.

995 Plan ahead for countdown to moving day.

✔ Organize and pack everything that's left to pack.

✔ Take down curtains, drapes, or blinds that are not staying with the house.

✔ Check attics, crawl spaces, basement, and garage for items that need to be packed, discarded, or given away.

✔ Find location for owner's manuals, warranties, and service providers related to house.

✔ Pick up dry cleaning.

✔ Order and pick up prescription medicines.

✔ Clean out freezer and refrigerator.

✔ Mow the lawn.

✔ Clean out litter boxes.

✔ Gather all sets of extra house keys from family, service providers, and neighbors.

✔ Leave three large postage-paid pre-addressed envelopes for the new owners to forward magazines or other items to your new address.

✔ Drain waterbeds.

✔ Knock down aquariums.

996 Consider what you shouldn't pack for moving day.

✔ Tools needed to break down furniture and appliances.

✔ Heavy-duty extension cords.

✔ Flashlights.

✔ Broom and dust pan.

✔ Vacuum cleaner.

✔ Trash bags.

✔ Duct tape.

997   Remember to create an essentials kit for your family that goes with you in transit.

✔ Change of clothes.

✔ Towels.

✔ Over-the-counter and prescription drugs.

✔ First aid kit.

✔ Toilet paper and paper towels.

✔ Trash and reclosable bags.

✔ Flashlight.

✔ Pen, pencils, and paper.

✔ Travel cups.

998   Consider all costs associated with a move before you decide to move yourself.

✔ Cost of rental truck, dollies, moving pads, boxes, gasoline, and insurance, as well as your time and sweat.

999   Study self-move truck packing techniques.

✔ Keep the heaviest items toward the front of truck.

✔ Load the truck from floor to ceiling.

✔ Tie off sections of load to stop load from shifting in transit.

✔ Load artwork, headboards along the truck walls.

✔ Load lighter boxes on top of heavier ones.

✔ Keep brooms, vacuum cleaners, and trash cans at back of truck.

1000   Remember some basics when hiring professional movers.

✔ Movers must be properly insured for their vehicles, your belongings, and their employees (i.e., workman's compensation).

✔ Insurance must be in place for the van lines and their agent.

1001 Understand that national moving companies have agents who represent them in local markets. These agents are affiliated with national van lines.

1002 Local agents perform local moves affiliated with national van lines.

1003 Ask for written estimates from all moving company representatives when they physically review the items they will move and/or pack.

✔ You have specific legal protections with a written estimate.

✔ Some movers will guarantee their estimate if they conduct a personal review of your household goods to be moved.

1004 Contact your Better Business Bureau to verify credentials of any moving company your are considering using.

1005 Research how moving costs for national moves are calculated.

✔ Weight of shipment.

✔ Time involved in transport of household goods.

✔ The cubic footage of the shipment.

✔ Any combination of the above.

1006 Consider how property restrictions can increase moving costs.

✔ Stairs or elevators.

✔ Street or driveway is to narrow for the moving van.

✔ Gas, water, or electric lines need to be disconnected.

1007 Verify how your mover will want to be paid.

✔ Cash or certified check.

✔ Credit card.

1008   Remember to keep some cost-effective national moving tips in mind.

✔ Request that your load be direct loaded with no storage in transit.

✔ Complete all household packing yourself.

1009   Be aware of the various forms of insurance on your household goods.

✔ Minimum included in moving cost is 25 to 70 cents per pound.

✔ Actual cash value. The purchase price minus depreciation.

✔ Replacement coverage minus deductible.

✔ Check with moving companies on insurance protections if you pack yourself.

1010   Recognize that you must document in writing all losses or damage.

✔ Check "Conditioned Inventory" at origin and destination.

✔ Conditioned inventory: a list of all household goods and their exact condition.

✔ You have nine months to file a claim against your mover.

1011   Consider taking photos or movies of all your household goods and their condition before your move.

1012   Become familiar with moving terms.

✔ *Advanced charges*: charges for services performed by someone other than the mover. A third party may perform these services at your request.

✔ *Agent*: a local moving company authorized to act on behalf of a national company.

✔ *Bill of lading*: the receipt for your goods and the contract for their transportation.

✔ *Carrier*: the moving company transporting your household goods.

✔ *Estimate, binding*: guarantee of the total cost of the move based upon the quantities and services shown on the estimate.

✔ *Estimate, nonbinding*: what your mover believes the cost will be, based upon the estimated weight of the shipment and additional services requested. Your final charges will be based upon the actual weight of your shipment, the services provided, and the tariff provisions in effect.

✔ *Flight charge*: a charge for carrying items up or down flights of stairs.

✔ *Guaranteed pickup and delivery service*: a service that guarantees pickup and delivery dates (the mover will provide reimbursement to you for delays).

✔ *High-value article*: items included in a shipment valued at more than $100 per pound ($220 per kilogram).

✔ *Line haul charges*: charges for the vehicle transportation portion of your move. These charges, if separately stated, apply in addition to the accessorial service charges.

✔ *Long carry*: a charge for carrying articles excessive distances between the mover's vehicle and your residence.

✔ *Order number*: the bill of lading number used to identify and track your shipment.

✔ *Peak season rates*: higher line haul charges applicable during the summer months, Memorial Day to Labor Day.

✔ *Pickup and delivery service*: separate transportation charges applicable for transporting your shipment between the storage-in-transit warehouse and your residence.

✔ *Shuttle service*: the use of a smaller vehicle to provide service to residences not accessible to the mover's normal line haul vehicles.

✔ *Storage-in-transit*: temporary warehouse storage of your shipment pending further transportation.

✔ *Surface Transportation Board*: U.S. Department of Transportation regulatory body of household goods carrier tariffs.

✔ *Tariff*: document that must contain rates, rules, regulations, classifications, or other provisions. It includes, an accurate description, the specific applicable rates, and service terms for services a mover offers to the public. The mover's tariff must be arranged in a way that allows the consumer to determine the exact rate(s) and service terms.

✔ *Valuation*: the degree of insurance value of a shipment. The valuation charge compensates the mover for assuming a greater degree of liability than is provided for in its base transportation charges.

✔ *Warehouse handling*: a charge may be applicable each time storage-in-transit service is provided.

1013 Understand how the 400N tariff protects the moving consumer by guaranteeing the following:

✔ Written and binding estimates.

✔ The consumer right to be present when shipment is weighed.

✔ Movers offer dispute resolution.

✔ Must have a minimum level of insurance on all property.

1014 Be realistic when moving with children.

✔ If moving locally consider taking children to friends or relatives for the day.

✔ Allow extra time for packing.

✔ Keep routines, toys, and books familiar.

✔ Set up children's rooms first.

✔ Find after-school activities to help children make new friends.

✔ If it feels right, allow older children to stay behind and finish school.

✔ Volunteer at new school to be a reassuring presence for younger children.

✔ Keep children informed of moving details from the beginning.

✔ Have children pack favorite photos, pajamas, and slippers for first night in new home.

✔ Have children memorize new address and phone numbers before move.

✔ Buy journals for children to record feelings and hopes.

1015 Learn how to move your computer.

✔ Make backup copies of all your files.

✔ Store and move original program and backup disks separate from your computer.

✔ Prepare your hard disk for moving by placing in park and lock position.

✔ Pack your computer in original box and materials.

✔ Remove ink cartridges from printer.

✔ Insert piece of paper in platen to secure.

1016 Consider waterbeds will require extra attention when moving.

✔ Determine which style mattress you have. Floating baffle, attached or nonbaffle, fiber, chambered, or cellular mattress.

✔ Rolling or folding? See your manufactures instructions.

✔ Do not attempt to unfold or roll frozen mattresses, allow them to return to room temperature first.

✔ Add a recommended waterbed cleaner to reduce bacterial growth before moving.

1017 Be realistic when self-moving a piano.

✔ Rent a piano dolly.

✔ Have at least four adults to move piano.

✔ Take extra care with fragile piano legs.

1018 Decide the best way to move your pets.

✔ Get copies of health records from veterinarian.

✔ Have identification and rabies tags secured to animal.

✔ Check leash laws in new community.

✔ Check with airline for policy and procedure for pet travel.

✔ If traveling by car verify lodging will accept pets.

✔ Maintain normal routines as much as possible.

1019 Recognize the requirements to move birds and fish.

✔ Birds need a health certificate to enter most states.

✔ Keep birds covered to prevent drafts and diminish stress.

✔ Do not allow movers to move fish tanks.

✔ Maintain even temperatures for fish.

✔ Long trips require battery-powered air pumps and air stones.

✔ Fish will not eat during moves.

1020 Determine whether you will need temporary storage.

✔ Temperature regulated.

✔ Access hours and days.

✔ Does homeowners insurance cover contents in temporary storage?

✔ Can you extend time in the same space?

1021 Study whether you should hire an auto-transporter service.

✔ Open or enclosed transport.

✔ Door-to-door or terminal-to-terminal.

✔ Is transporter's insurance primary or secondary to yours?

✔ Classic or exotic car.

✔ Extra cars in family.

✔ Motorcycles.

✔ Sport utility vehicles.

✔ Expect transport to take one week coast-to-coast.

✔ Remove bike or ski racks.

✔ Leave fuel tank only 1/4 full.

✔ Crack windows for ventilation.

✔ Inspect vehicle when picking up.

1022 Remember that you can have your household goods mover transport your car.

✔ Cost calculated by auto's weight and time and distance transported.

1023 Be prepared for your first night in your new home.

✔ Post an emergency phone list for your new community on your refrigerator.

✔ Change the locks.

✔ Change batteries in smoke detectors.

✔ Have flashlights handy.

✔ Check to see whether all blinds and shades operate correctly before nightfall.

1024 Assist your movers by labeling the rooms in your new home and write occupant's names on doors.

1025 Consider your basic needs on your first day in your new home.

✔ Set up the kitchen with basics. Coffee maker, cleaning supplies, dishes, pots and pans.

✔ Prepare the bathroom with toiletries, wastebasket, towels, and shower curtain.

✔ Connect telephone answering machine, computers, television sets, DVD, and VCRs.

✔ Set up and make beds.

✔ Unpack clothing. Set up alarm clock.

✔ Locate lamps and lightbulbs.

✔ Make a trip to grocery store for necessities.

Appendix A
MARK'S STORIES

Experienced But Knowledgeable?

At a new listing in a seller's market, I was holding a public open house. I had good traffic through the property. Near the end, an agent came with clients to see the house. The clients liked it, and the agent said she would write a contract. She returned shortly and presented an earnest money check and a written offer to me, without disclosures and without a prequalification letter for her buyers. I thanked her for the offer and said I would present it to my seller. I also added that the seller most likely would not respond without supporting documents stating that the buyers had the ability to close a loan for the property and the required signed disclosures. The agent became belligerent and asked whether I knew she had been in real estate sales for 25 years. She went on to say that with her reputation, her clients did not need to provide the seller with documentation of their ability to secure a mortgage for the property. I replied in a professional manner that I did not know her or her clients and that my seller did not know her or her clients, but we would like to pursue her offer if she provided the information necessary to make a decision. The agent said she would get back to me. She did. She provided the information, and we went to closing, but not without her continued grandstanding about her experience in real estate sales.

Agent's Money

Real estate agents talk openly among themselves about commission splits and how much the cooperating broker will pay on a property they just sold. But if a client asks how they are compensated and what the approximate amount they will receive on the purchase, the answer most likely will be short but not direct. Many people don't like to talk about money on a personal level. But as a client, if you look on your closing documents, it will be disclosed how much your agent is getting paid. You might be surprised to learn how much your agent was paid. The question is, did you feel that you received service equal to their compensation? When you're working with an agent don't be afraid to get a idea of what they will most likely make, then ask them to perform accordingly.

Allergies Can Kill a Showing

If you have allergies or are sensitive to unpleasant smells such as stale cigarette smoke, tell your agent before they make any appointments to show you homes. I had a client who was very allergic to cats and didn't tell me until we were viewing a property and two cats came around to check us out. He had an immediate allergic reaction and ran out of the house. The same buyer's partner did not want to view homes with dogs inside. I didn't know this until she froze on the front porch refusing to go in, even if I took the dog out the back door before she entered. Tell your agent these details before you go out for the first time to view properties so that you won't be wasting your time, the seller's time to prepare for a showing, or your agent's time.

"It Isn't Over Until It Is Closed"?

In the real estate business agents say that the transaction "Isn't over until it is closed." Very true, but sometimes agents call me a week before the closing to say they can't make it and could I get their documents and deliver them. I can't tell you how important it is for all of the transaction participants to be at the closing, to make sure that it goes smoothly and timely. Don't settle for "my job is done" or "it's in the attorney's hands now"; you never know when your agent might have keys, garage door openers, final meter readings, or was informed of something at the last minute that could impact the closing that they didn't share with you. They can be the extra pair of legs to go get the insurance binder or driver's license a client forgot to bring to closing. They get compensated through closing, so they should be there.

The Agent's Only as Good as the Managing Broker

Is your agent's managing broker punctual with appointments and returning phone calls? Does your agent's managing broker answer your questions completely, dress professionally and maintain a professional attitude, practice and respect real estate ethics, understand that real estate sales agents are no longer "keepers of information," and know that real estate sales agents must add value to the transactions of real estate? The answer should be yes to all.

Spend Ten Dollars to Save One

Finding a good, professional mortgage banker or broker is time and energy well spent. The time and frustration saved from finding a real mortgage pro early in your home search will make up in the possible 1/8-point interest rate difference. Clients of mine several years ago played the rate game, working and shopping to find the best rate for a 3% down mortgage. They called with what I thought was a "too good to be true" interest rate. I suggested that they look carefully at their good faith estimate and their truth in lending documents. They called back and said that there were no surprises there, so we moved forward toward the closing date. The day before closing one of the buyers called their attorney to find out how much money they needed to bring to closing. The attorney gave a number that sent my clients reeling. They called their mortgage broker and he informed them that they had to pay several thousand dollars in additional closing costs because they were only putting 3% down. My clients didn't have the extra money and were panic stricken. The mortgage contingency was long expired and they didn't know what to do. I told them to call their attorney and inform her what was going on. After several rounds between the attorneys for both the buyer and seller, the mortgage broker agreed to fund the loan and drop the last minute fees that were never disclosed in the Good Faith Estimate and Truth-in-Lending documents.

A Commitment Letter Is as Good as Cash

Most real estate agents and sellers feel a commitment letter for a mortgage is the equivalent of cash. By the time a commitment letter is issued the borrower has successfully completed the lender's requirements to be able to financially close the loan. On occasion when real estate contracts are submitted to a seller in a multiple offer situation, the agent with the cash offer feels it is the best offer. Remind the seller or your real estate agent that a loan commitment is the same as cash. Why I feel a commitment letter is better than cash is that a neutral third party has reviewed the buyer's ability to close the loan and thus the transaction. A cash buyer, unless they provide proof of funds to close the transaction with their offer, is really less qualified than a buyer with a loan commitment.

They've Come a Long Way in a Short Time
The Internet boom of several years ago brought online mortgage lenders and online applications to real estate consumers. My tech-savvy clients rushed to this new resource with mixed results. Early problems included mortgage processors and under-writers in faraway places that didn't understand the local market for appraisal, closing, or legal customs and practices. Although most of these wrinkles have been ironed out in the past couple of years, remember that online lenders are online and not always next door.

PMI: Easy as to Get out of as Into?
Most lenders want a productive relationship with their borrowers, but they don't always have the systems in place and the time to be as proactive for determining when a mortgage meets Homeowners Protection Act guidelines for release of mortgage insurance premiums. So if your lender doesn't know (especially if they are far away from your market) that your market is appreciating consistently, you need to educate them. You should hire an experienced licensed appraiser to independently verify home appreciation. If the appraisal confirms that appreciation now releases you from PMI insurance, contact your lender. I have seen in my market appreciation rates large enough to remove PMI in as little as one year.

Verify When Your Loan Is Sold, or You Could Double Pay
Some mortgage brokers only originate loans for companies that hold and service them. Some of these companies that hold or service them will sell them to another company to hold service them. Some companies that hold loans subcontract the serv-ice of these loans. If you receive a letter that your loan has been sold and you should send your payments to a new company or address, verify the change with your current mortgage company. Several mortgage scams have preyed upon mortgage consumers in recent years where the borrower receives an official-looking letter from their mortgage company stating that the borrowers' loan has been sold to X Company. The borrower, without verifying the change, starts sending mortgage payments to X Company while their original mortgage company is still expecting the borrowers' payments, because they did not sell the loan!

Appendix B
Helpful Checklists

1. Home Purchase Worksheet

	House 1 Date: Address:	House 2 Date: Address:	House 3 Date: Address:	Go Back 2nd Show?
Price				
Condo Fees (if applicable)				
Special Assessments				
Taxes				
# of Rooms				
# of Bedrooms				
# of Baths				
Master Bath				
Fireplace(s)				
Floor Plan				
Functionality				
Wall Condition				
Wallpaper				
Closet Space				
Storage				
Attic				
Kitchen Eat-in				
Appliances				
Countertops				
Laundry				
Garage/Parking				
Auto Opener				
Driveway				
Yard Size				
Fenced				
Roof Condition				
Windows				
Traffic				
Neighborhood				
Schools				
Curb Appeal				
Utility Costs				
Notes				
Distance to: Work Public Transportation Shopping Recreation Hospitals Trash Pickup Other:				

2. Professional Agent Profile

	Agent 1	Agent 2	Agent 3
Name of Firm			
Name of Man. Broker			
Man. Broker Phone #			
Name of Agent			
Phone Office # Cell # Pager #			
E-mail Address			
# of Years in Real Estate			
Full Time?			
Part Time?			
Vacations Planned?			
Communities Covered			
Number of Transactions			
Services Provided			
Firm Web site?			
Agent Web site?			
Member of Nat. Assoc.?			
Member State Assoc.?			
Member MLS			
Professional:			
Manner			
Appearance			
Attentive			
Home Office			
Assistant			
Laptop Computer			
Low/Med/High Pressure			
Friendly			
Professional Designation			
Relocation Certified			
Dual Agent			
Misc. Comments			

3. School Comparison Chart

	School 1	School 2	School 3	Notes
Name				
District				
Principal				
Address				
Telephone				
School Hours				
Transportation				
Student Class Size				
Grades at School				
Curriculum				
Nightly Homework				
How Students Graded				
# of Report Cards/Year				
Stand. Tests Given				
Special Education				
Gifted Education				
# Parent/Teacher Conf.				
Librarian				
Guidance Counselor				
Computers per Student				
Foreign Language				
Art Program				
Band Program				
Choir				
Theater Program				
Sports				
On-site Nurse				
Special Clubs/Assoc.				
After-School Care				
Cafeteria				
Dress Code				
Waiting List				

4. Basic Home Inspection Checklist

A professional, licensed home inspector should do your home inspection, however the following checklist can be used to note what the inspector may check.

	Good	Fair	Needs Attention/ Cost	Notes:
Foundation				
Grading				
Dampness				
Leaks				
Floor Drains				
Ventilation				
Exterior Walls				
Masonry				
Painted Surface				
Siding/Trim				
Soffits				
Roof				
House				
Porch				
Garage				
Other				
Gutters/Down				
Chimney				
Chimney Cap				
Antennas				
Vents/Louvers				
Doors/Windows				
Front Elevation				
Side 1 Elev.				
Side 2 Elev.				
Rear Elevation				
Garage				
Porch 1				
Porch 2				
Other				
Heat/Cooling				
Furnace				
A/C Condenser				
Humidifier				
Air Cleaner				
Hot Water Heater				

	Good	Fair	Needs Attention/ Cost	Notes:
Window Air 1				
Window Air 2				
Window Air 3				
Service History				
Air Filters				
Ceiling Fans				
Electrical				
Ground				
Main				
Sub Panels				
Circuit Breaker				
Fuses				
Service Size				
GFIs				
Kitchen				
Cabinets				
Countertops				
Floor				
Walls				
GFI				
Ceiling				
Exhaust Fans				
Appliances				
Stove				
Oven				
Microwave				
Cooktop				
Refrigerator				
Freezer				
Dishwasher				
Disposal				
Trash Compact				
Lighting/Light				
Bkfst Bar				
Table Space				
Pantry				
Living Room				
Fireplace				

5. Final Walk-Through Worksheet

Final Walk-Through Worksheet	Date: Time:		
Kitchen		**Master Bedroom**	
Refrigerator		Closets	
Freezer		Built-ins	
Dishwasher		Floors	
Stove		Walls	
Oven		Ceiling Fans	
Cooktop		Fireplace	
Microwave		Window A/C	
Disposal			
Trash Compactor		**Bedroom 2**	
Cabinets		Closets	
Drawers		Built-ins	
Pantry		Floors	
Lights		Walls	
Floors		Ceiling Fans	
Walls		Fireplace	
Ceiling Fans		Window A/C	
Window A/C			
		Bedroom 3	
Mechanical Systems		Closets	
Heating		Built-ins	
Cooling		Floors	
Humidifier		Walls	
Air Cleaner		Ceiling Fans	
Sump Pump		Fireplace	
Water Well Pump		Window A/C	
Hot Water Heater			
Washer		**Bedroom 4**	
Dryer		Closets	
Garage		Built-ins	
Auto Door		Floors	
Transmitter(s)		Walls	
Basement		Ceiling Fans	
Attic-House		Fireplace	
Attic-Garage		Window A/C	
Crawlspace			
Shed			
Bathroom 1			
Run Water Sink		**Bedroom 5**	
Flush Toilet		Closets	
Run Water Tub/Shw		Built-ins	

Final Walk-Through Worksheet	Date: Time:		
Check Med Cab		Floors	
Bath 2		Walls	
Run Water Sink		Ceiling Fans	
Flush Toilet		Fireplace	
Run Water Tub/Shw		Window A/C	
Check Med Cab.			
Linen Closet			
Bath 3		**Hall/Foyer/Entry 1**	
Run Water Sink		Closet	
Flush Toilet		Walls	
Run Water Tub/Shw		Floors	
Check Med Cab.			
Linen Closet			
Bath 4		**Hall/Foyer/Entry 2**	
Run Water Sink		Closet	
Flush Toilet		Walls	
Run Water Tub/Shw		Floors	
Check Med Cab.			
Linen Closet			
		Hall/Foyer/Entry 3	
Living Room		Closet	
Fireplace		Walls	
Built-ins		Floors	
Floor			
Walls			
Ceiling Fans		**Basement**	
Closet			
Window Coverings			
Window A/C			
		Porch	
Family Room			
Fireplace			
Built-ins		**Driveway**	
Floor			
Walls			
Ceiling Fans/ Window A/C		**Technology:** Cable Box	
Closet		**Recycling Boxes**	
Window Coverings			

Appendix C
Useful URLs

A

Accredited Buyer Representative (ABR)
http://www.rebac.net

Accredited Land Consultant
http://www.rliland.com

Accredited Residential Manager (ARM)
http://www.irem.org.

Alabama Association of REALTORS®
http://www.alabamarealtors.com

Alaska Association of REALTORS® Inc.
http://www.alaskarealtors.com

Americans with Disabilities Act
http://www.usdoj.gov/crt/ada/adahom1.htm

American Society of Farm Managers and Rural Appraisers
http://www.asfmra.org

American Society of Home Inspectors
http://www.ashi.com

AOL Home Price Check
http://aol.homepricecheck.com

The Appraisal Foundation
http://www.appraisalfoundation.org

Appraisal Institute
http://www.appraisalinstitute.org

Arkansas REALTORS® Association
http://www.arkansasrealtors.com

Arizona Association of REALTORS®
http://www.aaronline.com

Asbestos (U.S. Environmental Protection Agency)
http://www.epa.gov/asbestos/asbreg.html

B

Bank Rate Monitor
http://www.bankrate.com

Bankruptcy in Brief
http://www.bankruptcy-expert.com

Buy Owner
http://www.buyowner.com

C

California Association of REALTORS® Inc.
http://www.car.org

The Canadian Real Estate Association
http://www.crea.ca

Century 21
http://www.century21.com

Council of Residential Specialists (CRS)
http://www.crs.com

Certified International Property Specialist
http://www.cipsnetwork.com

Coldwell Banker
http://www.coldwellbanker.com

Colorado Association of REALTORS® Inc
http://www.colorealtor.org

Connecticut Department of Banking
http://www.state.ct.us/dob/

Consumer Publications
http://www.pueblo.gsa.gov

Countrywide Financial
http://www.countrywide.com

Crossroads Real Estate Referral Network
http://www.crossroadsrelocation.org

D

Delaware Association of REALTORS®
http://www.delawarerealtor.com

Department of Housing and Urban Development (HUD)
http://www.hud.org

Department of Veterans Affairs (VA)
http://www.va.gov

Doctor Locator
http://www.locateadoc.com

E

e-Bay Real Estate
http://pages.ebay.com/realestate/

Educated Home Buyer.com
http://www.educatedhomebuyer.com

E-Loan
http://www.eloan.com

Employee Relocation Council
http://www.erc.org

e-PRO
http://www.epronar.com/

ERA.com
http://www.era.com

Everything Real Estate.com
http://www.everythingre.com

F

Fair Housing Laws
http://www.hud.gov/offices/fheo/FHLaws/index.cfm

Fannie Mae
http://www.fanniemae.com

Feng Shui
http://www.wofs.com

Florida Manufactured Homes Magazine
http://www.mcxpress.com

For Sale By Owner
http://www.fsbo-easy.com

Freddie Mac
http://www.freddiemac.com

G

GMAC Real Estate
http://www.gmacre.com

Georgia Association of REALTORS®
http://www.garealtor.com

Graduate, REALTORS® Institute
http://www.edesignations.com

Green Building
http://www.nrg-builder.com

H

Hawaii Association of REALTORS®
http://www.hawaiirealtors.com

Homes.com
http://www.homes.com

Home Advisor
http://www.homeadvisor.com

Home Shark
http://www.homeshark.com

Homestead.com
http://www.homestead.com

Housing Trust Funds
http://www.nhtf.org

House Values.com
http://www.housevalues.com

HUD Department of Housing and Urban Development
http://www.hud.org

I

Idaho Association of REALTORS® Inc.
http://www.idahorealtors.com

ihouse 2000™
http://www.ihouse2000.com

Illinois Association of REALTORS®
http://www.illinoisrealtor.org

Illinois Office of Banks and Real Estate
http://www.obre.state.il.us/AGENCY/aboutobre.htm

Indiana Association of REALTORS® Inc.
http://www.indianarealtors.com

Inman Real Estate News
http://www.inman.com

Institute of Real Estate Management
http://www.irem.org

Insure.com
http://www.insure.com/index.html#homeowner

Insurance Company Ratings
http://www.ambest.com

International Real Estate Digest
http://www.ired.com

K

Kansas Association of REALTORS® Inc.
http://www.kansasrealtor.com

Keller Williams Realty
http://www.kellerwilliams.com

Kentucky Association of REALTORS®
http://www.kar.com

L

Land Journal
http://www.landjournal.com

Lead Hazard Information
http://www.hud.gov/offices/lead/

Lending Tree
http://www.lendingtree.com

Louisiana REALTORS®
http://www.larealtors.org

M

Magnet Street
http://www.magnetstreet.com

Maine Association of REALTORS®
http://me.realtorplace.com

Manufactured Housing Institute
http://www.mfghome.org

Manufactured Housing and Standards
http://www.hud.gov/offices/hsg/sfh/mhs/mhshome.cfm

MapQuest.com
http://www.mapquest.com

Maryland Association of REALTORS® Inc.
http://www.mdrealtor.org

Massachusetts Association of REALTORS®
http://www.marealtor.com

Michigan Association of REALTORS®
http://www.mirealtors.com

Minnesota Association of REALTORS®
http://www.mnrealtor.com

Mold (U.S. Environmental Protection Agency)
http://www.epa.gov/iaq/molds/moldresources.html

Mortgage Bankers Association
http://www.mbaa.org

Mortgage Credit Problems
http://www.mortgagecreditproblems.com

N

Mark Nash
http://www.marknashrealtor.com

National Apartment Association
http://www.naahq.org

National Association of Exclusive Buyer Agents
http://www.naeba.com

National Association of Home Builders
http://www.nahb.com

National Association of Mortgage Brokers
http://www.namb.org

National Association of REALTORS® NAR
http://www.realtor.com or http://www.realtor.org

National Association of Real Estate Appraisers
http://www.iami.org

National Association of Real Estate Brokers
http://www.nareb.com

National Center for Home Equity Conversion (NCHEC) Reverse Mortgages
http://www.Reverse.org

National Property Management Association
http://www.npma.org

National Relocation & Real Estate
http://www.rismedia.com

New Hampshire Association of REALTORS® Inc.
http://www.nhar.com

New Jersey Association of REALTORS®
http://www.njar.com

New York State Association of REALTORS® Inc.
http://www.nysar.com

North Carolina Association of REALTORS® Inc.
http://www.ncrealtors.org

North Dakota Association of REALTORS®
http://www.ndrealtor.com

O

Ohio Association of REALTORS®
http://www.ohiorealtors.org

Oklahoma Association of REALTORS®
http://www.oklahomarealtors.com

Online Mortgage Loans
http://www.lendingtree.com
http://www.quickenloans.com
http://www.wellsfargo.com/mortgage

Online Realty Sales.com
http://www.onlinerealtysales.com

Owners (Online real estate)
http://www.Owners.com

P

PrivateForSale.com
http://www.privateforsale.com

Prudential Real Estate
http://www.prudential.com

Q

Quicken Mortgage
http://www.quickenmortgage.com

R

Radon Information (U.S. Environmental Protection Agency)
http://www.epa.gov/iaq/radon/pubs/hmbyguid.html

Real Estate ABC
http://www.realestateabc.com

Real Estate Agencies.net
http://www.realestateagencies.net

Real Estate Auction Guide.com
http://www.realestateauctionguide.com

Real Estate Café
http://www.realestatecafe.com

Real Estate.com
http://www.realestate.com

Real Estate Directory
http://www.realestate4.com/

The Real Estate Library
http://www.relibrary.com

Realty Times
http://www.realtytimes.com

Rebuz.com
http://www.rebuz.com

Re/Max.com
http://www.remax.com

Rhode Island Association of REALTORS® Inc.
http://www.riliving.com

S

School Information
http://www.school match.com
http://www.theschoolreport.com

School Statistics: National Center For Education Statistics
http://www.nces.ed.gov/globallocator

Seniors Real Estate Specialist
http://www.seniorsrealestate.com

Society of Industrial and Office REALTORS®
http://www.sior.com

South Carolina Association of REALTORS®
http://www.screaltors.com

South Dakota Association of REALTORS®
http://www.sdrealtor.org

T

Tennessee Association of REALTORS®
http://www.tarnet.com

Texas Association of REALTORS®
http://www.texasrealtors.com

U

U.S. Postal Service Moving Guide
http://www.usps.com/moversguide

Urban Development
http://www.hud.gov

Utah Association of REALTORS®
http://www.utahrealtors.com

V

VA, Department of Veteran Affairs
http://www.va.gov

Vandema Commercial Real Estate Resources
http://www.vandema.com

Vermont Association of REALTORS® Inc.
http://www.vtrealtor.com

Virginia Association of REALTORS®
http://www.varealtor.com

Virtual Relocation
http://www.virtualrelocation.com

W

Warranties, Homeowners
http://www.americanhomeshield.com

Washington Mutual Home Loans
http://www.wamu.com

Wells Fargo Home Loans
http://www.wellsfargo.com

Wisconsin REALTORS® Association
http://www.wra.org

Women's Council of REALTORS®
http://www.wcr.org

Y

Yahoo! Real Estate
http://list.realestate.yahoo.com